LIVING ARCHITECTURE

LIVING ARCHITECTURE
A BIOGRAPHY OF H. H. RICHARDSON

JAMES F. O'GORMAN
PHOTOGRAPHS BY CERVIN ROBINSON

SIMON & SCHUSTER EDITIONS

To the descendants of H. H. Richardson who have
continued the "family business"

◆

SIMON & SCHUSTER EDITIONS
Rockefeller Center
1230 Avenue of the Americas
New York, NY 10020

SIMON & SCHUSTER EDITIONS and colophon are trade-
marks of Simon & Schuster Inc.

Designed by Susan E. Kelly, Marquand Books, Inc., Seattle

Manufactured in Italy

10 9 8 7 6 5 4 3 2 1

Library of Congress Cataloging-in-Publication Data

O'Gorman, James F.
    Living architecture : a biography of H. H. Richardson/
    James F. O'Gorman ; photographs by Cervin Robinson.
       p.   cm
    Includes bibliographical references and index.
    1. Richardson, H. H. (Henry Hobson), 1838–1886.
    2. Architects—United States—Biography. I. Richardson,
    H. H. (Henry Hobson), 1838–1886. II. Robinson, Cervin.
    III. Title.
    NA737.R5038   1997
    720'.92—dc21   97-20534
    [B]   CIP

ISBN 0-684-83618-1

HALF TITLE: *Carriage entrance, Old Colony Railroad Depot,
North Easton, Massachusetts, 1881–84.*

FRONTISPIECE: *West front of Trinity Church, Copley Square,
Boston, 1872–77.*

TITLE PAGE: *Exterior detail of the Old Colony Railroad Depot,
North Easton, Massachusetts, 1881–84.*

PAGE 6: *Main stairway of the Allegheny County Courthouse,
Pittsburgh, 1883–88.*

Although there is plenty of space on a gravestone to contain,
bound in moss, the abridged version of a man's life,
detail is always welcome.

V. NABOKOV, *Laughter in the Dark*

◆

CONTENTS

·ANNO DOMINI·
·MDCCCLXXXI·

1 ❖ CINCINNATI 1885

THE TWO MEN WHO STEPPED DOWN FROM A WEST-
bound train at Central Union Depot in Cincinnati that Janu
ary day in 1885 presented a study in contrast. One looked as
slim as a nail; the other, as big as a house. They were architects, and they had come in search of a job.

Lanky George Shepley, then in his mid-twenties, had
left a St. Louis family with deep New England roots to study
architecture at Boston's Massachusetts Institute of Technology. He had recently joined the nearby office of his traveling
companion, Henry Hobson Richardson, and quickly become
his trusted right-hand man. Shepley was to marry the boss's
daughter shortly after Richardson's death, in the spring of
the following year, and share the lead in the firm that suc-

H. H. Richardson, caricature of himself, his assistant George Shepley, and a porter, in a letter to his wife datelined Cincinnati, January 27, 1885. The imposing architect, here leading the parade, matched his imposing buildings. (Department of Printing and Graphic Arts, Houghton Library, Harvard University, Cambridge, Massachusetts)

ceeded to Richardson's practice. The older architect was obviously fond of the
young man, and Shepley's admiration for his mentor took visible form on this trip
in his copying of Richardson's well-cut suit, derby hat, and walking stick, although Richardson's full beard found only a diminished reflection in Shepley's
brushy mustache.

Leader of the parade was H. H. Richardson himself. Beneath his derby hat
he sported dark hair parted in the middle, an untrimmed beard, sparkling eyes,
and a bulbous nose. He was in his mid-forties, somewhere near six feet tall, and
weighed well over three hundred pounds. His tent-sized suit enveloped an enormous girth, inadequately supported by his slender cane. An impediment turned
his speech into the sound of a Gatling gun. "A mournful object for size" is how
one client described him, although his personality was anything but doleful. A
younger colleague recalled that he had a big mind in a big body, and so genial and
kindly and delightful a manner that everyone he met yielded to his infectious
enthusiasm. His friend Henry Adams said that he embodied such an "overflow of
life" that he was "irresistible."

The architect stood at the peak of his career in 1885; he bestrode his profession as its most colorful and influential member. Born on a Louisiana plantation,
educated at Harvard College in Massachusetts and the École des Beaux-Arts in
Paris, he had in less than two decades become the architect to watch, America's

OPPOSITE: *Exterior detail, Crane Memorial Library, Quincy, Massachusetts, 1880–82. Dedham granite ashlars set in red mortar, East Longmeadow sandstone trim, a Romanesque arcade, carved ornamental accents (including an emblematic crane): such a vignette summarizes the amplitude of Richardsonian materialism.*

first "signature" architect. During the spring of this year his colleagues nation-wide picked what they thought were the ten best buildings in the country. Works by Richardson took up half the list, published in June, and his Trinity Church on Copley Square in Boston headed the lot. This was a man who clearly warranted the label of "distinguished architect" that the Cincinnati papers hung on him.

Richardson attained the status of premier architect in his own day and has retained that reputation in ours. A member of that generation of giants who brought American culture to maturity during the 1870s, a generation that included architects, writers, and artists such as Mark Twain and Winslow Homer, he established a kind of apostolic architectural succession that embraced Louis Sullivan and Frank Lloyd Wright. Like theirs, his work stood out in both character and quality from that of his contemporaries. He was the first of the trio to define American architecture as distinct from its European origins, as rooted in the cities and landscape of North America, and his work, like that of his successors, continues to attract acclamation throughout the world.

The architect brought freshness to American building. He saw history as precedent to be creatively interpreted rather than authority to be blindly followed. His mature work was characterized by attention to the elements of architecture rather than to historical accuracy: to generous spaces, monumental forms, natural materials such as granite or shingles, broad openings, the studied relationship between simple solids and repetitive voids, sheltering roofs, massive chimneys, and a control of silhouette that was so different from the busy Victorian designs of his contemporaries. Unlike theirs, his works were imposingly solid. There was an amplitude in his use of materials unmatched in their dry designs. His buildings seem permanent fixtures on their sites. Richardson gave particular attention to environment, to the relationship of architecture to landscape; and even today a visitor to one of his buildings senses a timeless quality, an inevitable presence, a feeling that it has always been there.

Richardson earned the commissions upon which his lasting reputation rests through the originality of his talent and the force of his personality. His visit to Cincinnati exemplifies both of these characteristics at the height of his career.

His stature as an architect of parts was well established by 1885. In Cincinnati he immediately attracted the attention of his local colleagues, who called in numbers at his lodgings in the comfortable St. Nicholas Hotel, at Fourth and Race Streets in the center of the city. The St. Nicholas occupied an austere block—foursquare, four-storied, stone-faced, with a Greek Ionic portico—built in the stringent midcentury architectural style. Such earlier work had caught Richardson's eye during his student days, but he had left that mode far behind in his mature practice.

The members of the local press flocked around him, too, and the columns that resulted were altogether admiring. "They have made much of me," Richard-

son wrote his wife, Julia, who was home with the six children in suburban Brookline, Massachusetts. A reporter from the *Commercial Gazette* described the architect of Trinity Church (which he called "the most beautiful structure on this continent") as striking in personal appearance, so striking that it required italics to do him justice. Richardson was *large and portly,* with a *fine, full face, beaming with good nature.* He looked like an English aristocrat. In a later article, a reporter from the rival *Enquirer* also found it necessary to use italics in describing the architect, as if any personal reference required bombast. This writer resorted to architectural simile, describing to his readers a corpulent gentleman who *"wears a bay window nearly as large as the chamber itself will be."* It was a commonplace of the day that the architect resembled his imposing buildings, and that they reflected his monumental presence. In this case, the reporter had in mind the projected Cincinnati Chamber of Commerce building, the reason for Richardson's visit.

Cincinnati was approaching its centennial when Richardson arrived. Its location on the Ohio River had made it the major city of the opening Midwest, a cultural center in the 1820s and 1830s, when the Trollopes and the Beechers

Interior of Trinity Church, Copley Square, Boston, 1872–77. At the time of its completion, Trinity was considered the most beautiful church in America. It still ranks near the top in listings of the country's best buildings.

H. H. Richardson in Washington, D.C., ca. 1884. This photograph by Marian Hooper "Clover" Adams, the wife of Henry Adams, shows a puffiness of the architect's features that may have been a symptom of Bright's disease.

made their homes there. It had contributed in a major way to the Union cause during the Civil War, and many of its leading citizens retained honorary military titles. More recently it had withstood trials by flood and riot. A record rise of the Ohio early in 1883 caused extensive hardship. The Chamber of Commerce appointed a relief committee headed by its president, Henry C. Urner, and soup kitchens appeared. Just a year later the Court House Riot broke out against a corrupt city government supported by an equally corrupt judicial system. Henry Urner then led the campaign to restore the city's self-confidence by reconstructing the courts building, gutted during the melee.

Having weathered trials by flood and fire, Cincinnati, along with the rest of the industrialized North, entered a period of economic hopefulness. In the 1880s —the first decade of great city building in the United States—the city's Chamber of Commerce reflected the prevailing attitude in its own reorganization and growth. And reorganization and growth often translate into architecture. In December 1884 the chamber's Board of Real Estate Managers announced a limited competition for the design of the Chamber of Commerce building, among six architectural firms: three local and three, including the nationally famous Richardson's, from outside the city. Five weeks later, on his way from Boston to Chicago, where his great Marshall Field Wholesale Store was under consideration, Richardson, with Shepley in tow, stopped to discuss the project with members of the building committee. He wanted to meet them face-to-face.

The chamber's administrative officer and statistician, Col. Sidney Maxwell —then in his fifties, sober, efficient, and churchy, his head full of the data of productivity—briefed Richardson on the building program. Four years later he would write the heartening nondenominational "hymn" sung at the dedication of this capitalist headquarters: "Within these walls of strength and grace,/May honor find a dwelling place." The architect needed and wanted the colonel's input, but he could have stayed in Brookline and received the facts by mail. Richardson's real reason for coming to town was to turn his beaming personality upon the members of the chamber who formed the building committee and would ultimately pick the winning design.

The committee included civic, business, and cultural leaders, the builders of the Queen City of the West. On it sat men like the president of the chamber, tireless fifty-five-year-old Henry Urner, then head of the National Insurance Company, as well as newspaperman James M. Glenn, "who had studied architecture and construction in early life," Gen. Andrew Hickenlooper, president of the Cincinnati Gas and Electric Company and former lieutenant governor of Ohio, and Capt. William W. Peabody, president of the Ohio and Mississippi Railroad. They were good fellows all. Obituaries remembered Urner, a charter member and erstwhile president of the swanky Queen City Club, as an agreeable companion noted for his genial social temperament. Richardson soon found himself at table with these fine chaps, and at table the architect's charm could be particularly irresistible. As another of his clients, the acute social observer Marian Hooper Adams, wrote, he could say, "'I am my own music,' for he carries off any dinner more or less gaily."

The ample male midsection loomed large in the period of material abundance that followed the Civil War, an era that has come to be called the Gilded Age. It was the inevitable result of monumental, many-course meals, and it incorporated the conspicuous consumption of the urban elite. While it betokened high living, however, it also fronted deep-seated problems. The Victorian life span fell short of today's, and that was especially true in Richardson's case. His enormous girth resulted in part from chronic nephritis, then called Bright's disease, a disorder of the kidneys that would kill him fifteen months later. But if he could prevent it, Richardson never allowed his uncertain health to dictate either his social or his professional activities, although the two were in fact much the same.

The reporter for the *Gazette* wrote that the architect enjoyed equally "*the pleasures of art and appetite.*" Richardson was a man's man, a hail-fellow-well-met whose love of food, drink, and male companionship reached Falstaffian proportions. In his letter to Julia he feigned embarrassment at so much attention and hospitality, but he also fairly crowed about lunches and carousing with the "jolly fellows" who held membership in the chamber. They took him to dine at the respectable, many-bayed and many-gabled redbrick Queen City Club, a picturesque architectural pile whose thin, nervous forms Richardson's own robust work had made obsolete. And they guided him to lower—or at least more informal—haunts as well. Long business lunches preceded visits to the city's saloons.

Following one lunch, Richardson shopped for some serious, if eclectic, literature—Marcus Aurelius, John Morse's new book on John Adams, and William Gill's life of Edgar Allan Poe—but he scarcely had time to read. In Cincinnati his minutes were fully occupied. Presbyterian Sidney Maxwell seems to have had better things to do, but there were plenty of men to show the visitor a good time after hours. Abandoning the colonel, Richardson and the always present Shepley joined a group of fellows at the club, including the maltster Herman Goepper, then in his late thirties. From there they attended a play and finally visited a "musical lager beer saloon" where an "all-girl" orchestra played "pretty good music."

Reading room, Crane Memorial Library, Quincy, Massachusetts, 1880–82. The Crane interior exudes the air of a nineteenth-century men's clubhouse, but it continues to serve a more diverse readership.

OPPOSITE: *Reading-room fireplace, Crane Memorial Library, Quincy, Massachusetts, 1880–82. With its handcrafted andirons, paneled and carved woodwork, and stained-glass windows, the Crane Library evokes the preindustrialized era that also inspired William Morris in England.*

Richardson got back to his rooms at the St. Nicholas about midnight and "slept like a top."

The architect does not locate the saloon in his letter to Julia, but, escorted by a German-American in the brewing business, he probably ended up somewhere in Cincinnati's famed Over-the-Rhine area. Saloons enlivened the district, as one guidebook described it, with plenty of foaming seidels, German cuisine, and Teutonic music. As a student at Harvard in the 1850s, Richardson had surely joined his mates in crawling through the lager beer saloons of Boston, but now, as a gentleman, he probably thought of the visit as mild slumming. Slumming or not, the architect seems to have taken to it as a fish to water. He even found it worth reporting to his wife.

Richardson reveled in such hearty male companionship. He joined more of the "boys" at the Hengstenberg Lunch Table, a meeting that brought together a jovial group of the city's commercial leaders. Urner was again present, as was Goepper. So were John Church, head of a piano company and a music publisher; John Stettinius, a member of the illustrious Longworth family and president of the Children's Home; Col. Leopold Markbreit, lawyer and journalist; and Gen. A. T. Goshorn, who had been honored by Queen Victoria for his work as director general of the Philadelphia Centennial Exposition in 1876.

The gathering included other members of the city's elite as well. William Watts Taylor, experienced cotton broker and "gentleman of culture," also showed up. Taylor had recently been named manager of the city's emerging Rookwood Pottery, founded in 1880 by Maria Longworth Nichols and located up on the crest of Mount Adams. The pottery stood in the vanguard of the reaction against industrialized arts and the preference for handicraft (or apparently handicraft) production that came to be called the Arts and Crafts Movement. Richardson had in recent years visited William Morris at the center of Arts and Crafts ideas in England, and met the famous ceramist William De Morgan, and at some time during his Cincinnati visit must have ridden the inclined railway to the Tudor-style building housing the pottery. An itemized inventory of his belongings made just after his death lists several pieces of "Cincinnati ware."

The architect was Southern born but had avoided the Civil War by staying in Paris in the early 1860s. Ohio had been a hotbed of Union sentiment during the war, so in Cincinnati he might have received a potentially chilly reception. From Generals Hickenlooper and Goshorn to Colonels Markbreit and Maxwell to

Captain Peabody, these men had volunteered and fought bravely for the North. Hickenlooper joined Sherman on his march; Markbreit survived more than a year in the Confederacy's infamous Libby Prison. But class is thicker than blood, it seems, and social ease and a magnetic personality will nullify old animosities. The architect's neutrality during the conflict did not become an issue. What's more, with fellows like Taylor, also Louisiana born and Harvard educated, Bellamy Storer, also Harvard educated and part of Richardson's Cincinnati culinary circle, and others who were too young to carry a grudge, Richardson, here as throughout his career, found support in congenial old school ties. And there was young Larz Anderson, another member of the Longworth clan, on vacation from his studies at Harvard, the son of Nicholas, Richardson's old Cambridge classmate, for whom he had designed a house in Washington. The architect rarely missed an opportunity to engage socially with clients, near clients, or potential clients.

At one of Richardson's visits the Hengstenberg Table met on the porch of the fashionable clubhouse next to the lake at the center of the Cincinnati Zoo. This was a three-story Italianate limestone block surrounded by verandas. Like the Queen City Club, it must have looked decidedly old-fashioned to Richardson's eye. Photographs exist of this memorable occasion, and they tell us much about the relationship between the architect and his clients and potential clients. In one the group stands in two rows along a fence, with Richardson in profile in the center and Shepley, as always, hovering in his vicinity. Table members Pitts Burt and Herman Goepper flank the guest and slyly spread themselves just far enough apart to expose the profile of his monumental midsection, where "the equator of the waistcoat meets the meridian of the pants."

In another photo the fellows have arranged themselves in four tiers on steps rising toward the clubhouse porch and the waiting lunch table. Richardson sits at the top in the center, a majestic finial to the composition, a mound of a man with parted hair, full beard, and puffy hands folded above derby and cane. He gazes out with twinkling eyes, clearly satisfied with the arrangement. King of the hill. Master of all he surveys. Or, more cogently, angler for the fish schooled below. It was a hierarchy that suited him. The English author Osbert Sitwell tells us that his father thought of the relationship between the patron and the artist as that of a bone to a dog or a mouse to a cat, "placed before him to be worried, gnawed, and teased." Richardson would have agreed. One client complained that the architect had a ring in his nose, could lead him around where he wanted, and was the "only man who could ever do that." At just this moment Richardson's friends and Washington clients John Hay and Henry Adams were consoling each other—only half in jest—for being "in his awful hands."

Richardson molded clients and potential clients as the Rookwood potters shaped clay. The evidence here is overwhelming. One obituary remembered him as "a master of men as well as of his art. . . . He moved them almost as he willed."

His daughter Julia Shepley recalled that he enjoyed "the joke of outwitting them." His friend and professional colleague Peter B. Wight characterized him as "strong in argument, mighty in his own convictions, and irresistible in expressing them." One of Richardson's chief assistants, Charles A. Coolidge, remembered a time when the architect found amusement by treating him as a client and leading him on from wanting a cottage to building a castle. He remembered too the comment of a New York state senator, who encountered Richardson when he was working at the Albany State house, that the architect would "charm a bird out of a bush." In Cincinnati in 1885, the "bird" was the commission for the Chamber of Commerce building.

The Hengstenberg fellows assume a sober mien in these photographs of their meeting with Richardson, but that was clearly for public display. They printed memoirs of their meetings in prolonged doggerel, meetings that were congenial, jovial, and wet. They customarily demanded of a guest of honor that he drink "as a bumper" a capacious loving cup full of beer. Few if any ever managed the feat. Richardson astonished the assembly, we learn from Charles Coolidge, as he took the brimful cup, squared himself, sipped, then drank it down . . . and drained the cup again! When Richardson departed Cincinnati he left in his wake a well-remembered reputation among the business elite of the city as a grand fellow who could down the beer.

H. H. Richardson (top) with members of the Hengstenberg Lunch Table, Cincinnati, 1885. The architect reigns over a group of potential clients.

The architect so impressed the Hengstenbergs with this performance that they had a replica of the loving cup made up at the Rookwood Pottery and shipped it to Brookline with an accompanying piece of doggerel. This displayed hearty camaraderie and creative allusion, as it confused for the sake of rhyme the ancient Greek god of goats with that of drink, and mixed in a French Renaissance giant to boot. It hailed the mighty thirst of "Bostonian Pan!" who "with kindly grace Gargantuan" had emptied "twice our sacramental chalice at a thrice." They may not have known that there was nothing unusual in his performance. Richardson's friend and collaborator the artist John La Farge described the architect as a "mighty eater and drinker—a pitcher of milk, a pitcher of champagne, a pitcher of water—everything was done on a large scale."

Appetite served art. The first order of business for an architect is to get the commission. Without that, nothing. And, competition or not, that was Richardson's Cincinnati agenda. He visited the city to impress not only his colorful personality but his architectural talents upon the men who would choose the winner of the competition for the merchants' exchange. He balanced fact-filled Colonel Maxwell with fun-filled Henry Urner and Herman Goepper. He not only gleaned information about what the chamber wanted; he convinced the board to agree to some of his own rules for the competition. Richardson wanted the drawings to remain his property (a sticky issue between architects and clients in this early era of professionalism), and he wanted the winner to have the execution of the work. He succeeded completely. As he told Julia, he had accomplished everything he had come for, and had a "*very* pleasant time" to boot.

Richardson was right to be satisfied with himself. During the spring he (and his assistants) prepared his competition entry back in his drafting rooms in Massachusetts and sent the drawings to Cincinnati. He returned to the city in June to await the board's decision at the Grand Hotel, at Fourth and Central Streets, near the proposed site of the new chamber. The Grand, described in its advertising as "one of the great hotels in the country," with the "largest and most imposing" lobby in the United States, occupied a rather bland, six-story structure in the French Neo-Grec style that Richardson had occasionally used in his early work but had quickly outgrown. It is the fate of outstanding architects to be always surrounded by run-of-the-mill buildings.

Richardson was laid up in his rooms at the Grand Hotel under the care of a Dr. Whitaker when he heard that he had won the commission. The result disgusted the local competitors, but they got it only half right when they grumbled that his social skills rather than the merit of his design had earned him the nod. It was, as usual, a powerful mixture of both.

It is one thing to attract attention, another to merit it. The jolly fellows of the chamber's Real Estate Board might have been swayed in part by the man's beaming personality, but they were also hard-nosed capitalists, and they must have thought Richardson's design struck just the right note in both function and form. Pan had succeeded at the drafting board as well as the luncheon table. The members of the chamber must have sought an efficient building as well as a landmark. They wanted it to work well, and they wanted it to be the architectural embodiment of what they hoped was, or would appear to be, the solidity of Cincinnati business. This may have been a nervous hope, for the national economy actually experienced a long depression from 1873 to the late 1890s, and they may have seen Richardson's substantial design as a bastion raised against the reality of economic stagnation. His plan promised to be serviceable, and his exterior looked like a bulwark. It appeared conservative and virile, and that was surely what sold them on it.

The chamber occupied a broadly rectangular lot fronted by three streets in the heart of downtown Cincinnati. Richardson's winning plans show how easily he organized the essentials of the building program into an efficient pattern. He divided the site into two zones: utility stack and commercial spaces. He placed the first zone—toilets, elevators, and other mechanical equipment, as well as stairs and other circulatory patterns that made the second usable—at the rear of the lot, adjacent to neighboring buildings, because there was little need for windows there. The second, or principal, zone, occupying three-quarters of the lot and lighted naturally from three sides, contained the vast Exchange Hall on the second floor, shops at ground level, and offices above. This exemplified French planning at its best. The primary division of the program into what the twentieth-century Philadelphia architect Louis I. Kahn called "served" and "servant" spaces directly reflected the rational planning principles Richardson had absorbed in the 1860s as a student at the École des Beaux-Arts, in Paris.

For the exterior Richardson offered variant designs. Both, according to the ever-inquisitive newspapers, which were obviously quoting the architect, depended for effect on the accentuation of main features (those representing the building's "leading purposes") and possessed the sense of solidity "requisite in dignified monumental work" by the "perfectly quiet and massive treatment" of the walls. This echoed, by the way, identical descriptions of the architect's concurrent designs for Chicago and Pittsburgh. The Chamber of Commerce, its exterior altered by further review and its dedication coming after Richardson's death, was finished by his loyal successors, the firm of Shepley, Rutan and Coolidge, and built

Courtyard, Allegheny County Courthouse, Pittsburgh, 1883–88. In the mid-1880s Richardson was at the apex of his career, responding with superb designs to commissions from Pittsburgh, Cincinnati, Chicago, and other midwestern cities.

by his favorite contractor, Norcross Brothers of Worcester, Massachusetts. It featured his signature random ashlar granite stonework and his signature Romanesque Revival style.

The chamber formed an imposing monument to Gilded Age capitalism. Sturdy, heavy walled, rising from the street with bulky corner towers to a precipitous roof, it externally revealed its leading purpose by a series of great round arches at the level of the exchange floor. It loomed manly, brawny, and distinctive in a conservative way. In this it aptly reflected both its designer and its occupants. The building seemed just right for its time, place, and purpose. Although few architectural critics of the twentieth century have considered it among Richardson's finest works, preoccupied as they have been with architecture that seemed *ahead of* rather than *of* its time, the author Charles Dudley Warner, who with Mark Twain wrote the novel that gave the Gilded Age its name, got it just right in 1889 when he called it "massive, medieval, challenging attention, and compelling criticism to give way to genuine admiration."

In Cincinnati in 1885, H. H. Richardson stood at the top of his profession. He owned a national reputation as the single most admired and emulated architect in America, and he appeared as fully in control of the process of seducing potential clients as he was in the designing of landmark buildings. His colorful personality, enormous appetite, forceful presence, magnetic charm, virile persona, and apparently endless curiosity and energy were all in evidence, as was his architectural genius. Also evident was the fatal flaw in his physical makeup, his terminal disease. In his maturity Richardson's life fluctuated between professional success and physical distress, and he would expire at the moment of his greatest triumphs, in what most of us think of as middle age, just over forty-seven years after his birth.

OPPOSITE: *H. H. Richardson, Cincinnati Chamber of Commerce Building, 1885–88. This now-demolished building was a definitive work of the Richardsonian Romanesque.*

2 ❖ NEW ORLEANS 1838–55

A COMBINATION OF SOUTHERN GRACE AND NORTHERN energy. that's how one of Richardson's chief assistants summed up the architect; and indeed, he was shaped during his first twenty-one years by such disparate places as Louisiana and Massachusetts. But the story of Richardson's life begins in England, not the United States. It begins in the eighteenth century, not the nineteenth. And it begins with expatriation and attempted patricide.

According to his friend and client the Reverend Phillips Brooks, Richardson loved to boast that he was descended from Dr. Joseph Priestley, who is often credited with the discovery of oxygen. We know he bragged about his ancestry to a fellow boarder in a Brooklyn rooming house in 1866, and he mentioned it to an English clergyman he met casually in a carriage near Burgos in Spain in the summer of 1882. He was obviously proud of the fact, but he was prob-ably not aware of the full history of his descent. That did not become generally known until revealed by Priestley's modern biographer.

Joseph Priestley was born 105 years before Richardson and grew up to become one of the noted intellectuals of the eighteenth century. He was both scientist and theologian, and his experiments and publications on electricity, gases, light, and a bewildering array of other subjects earned him an important place in the history of science. His greatest achievements in this field were, perhaps, his discovery that air was a mixture of gases, including oxygen (although he left it to the Frenchman Antoine Lavoisier to call it that), and his recognition of the role of oxygen in the animal-plant metabolic process.

Dr. Priestley's friend Benjamin Franklin called him an "honest heretic." He was an independent thinker, a nonconformist in religion who helped found Unitarianism, a dissenter in politics who championed the principles of the American and French Revolutions, and a foe of the slave trade. Such opinions were unpopular in England, and they got him into trouble. His political position, especially, offended his countrymen, who, having watched their American colonies slip away in one revolution, were wary of the unsettling developments across the channel. After a dinner in Birmingham in 1791 called by a group of Francophiles to com-

Rembrandt Peale, Joseph Priestley, 1801. Priestley, the "discoverer" of oxygen and a founder of Unitarianism, was H. H. Richardson's maternal great-grandfather. (New-York Historical Society, New York City)

OPPOSITE: *Reading-room fireplace, Oliver Ames Memorial Library, North Easton, Massachusetts, 1877–78. The Ameses were pre–Civil War manufacturers of tools that were shipped across the United States and sold in outlets such as that of Priestley and Bein in New Orleans, Richardson's family's hardware store. After the war, they became Richardson's most important clients.*

Exterior detail, Oliver Ames Memorial Library, North Easton, Massachusetts, 1877–78. The cock carved on the impost of the entrance arch gives a wake-up call just as the owl on the pendant impost seems to admonish the reader to get wise.

celebrants, expressed its fears and frustrations by sacking and burning Priestley's house. Although he and his family escaped unharmed, his wife was shaken by the experience. "So much for King and Church forever," she wrote.

Priestley's life in England proved increasingly difficult during the next year or two. He became, for example, the subject of vicious political cartoons. In one of 1793 by James Gillray he is shown with other dissenters wearing a revolutionary, Jacobin cap and treasonably offering the head of Prime Minister William Pitt and a broken royal crown to a grotesque French military figure. Joseph had accepted French citizenship, and he might have moved to France as well except that he, too, was wary of events there. Two of his sons had moved to America in 1793, so in April 1794 he sailed with the rest of his family on board the *Sansom* for New York.

By July they were in Philadelphia, then the seat of government of the new United States. Joseph created the first permanent Unitarian congregation in the New World in the capital city. The present Unitarian church on Walnut Street was designed by H. H. Richardson's contemporary Frank Furness. Within its walls is a tablet of Siena marble dedicated to the memory of Dr. Priestley, executed in Boston from the design of Andrews, Jacques and Rantoul—appropriately enough, for both Robert D. Andrews and Herbert Jacques were trained in the office of Priestley's great-grandson.

There was much Richardson had in common with his illustrious ancestor. They shared a gift for mathematics; both played the flute; both were good horsemen; both spoke in a rapid stutter. And both seemed to have had winning ways, for it was said of Priestley that, despite his many public battles over his views on science, religion, and politics, "he charmed away the bitterest prejudices in personal intercourse," while Richardson was noted for his ability to bewitch his clients. "He could make a friend of his worst enemy in five minutes," according to one obituary. Joseph Priestley's convictions about religion, however, did not descend unwatered to his great-grandson. Although Unitarianism was to play an important role in the beginning of the architect's career, he was apparently tolerant in but largely indifferent to doctrinal matters.

Joseph Priestley and Mary Wilkinson had four children. Like his father, the third child and second son, William, accepted French citizenship and became a member of the bar in France the year after the Birmingham riot. Because he was his father's son and shared his father's political sympathies, he too became the subject of graphic ridicule in England. A cartoon by James Sayers published in 1792 shows "Monsieur François" dangling William Priestley before the French

*Entrance front, Oliver Ames Memorial Library,
North Easton, Massachusetts, 1877–78. Libraries
such as this represented a flowering of popular
education in the post–Civil War era and a new
spirit of public philanthropy.*

Assembly. Given the climate of fear and animosity between England and France at the time, his French adventure was an act of defiance to his homeland and another gesture hurrying along the family's expatriation.

Young William, H. H. Richardson's grandfather, was nothing like the son of another Mary and Joseph. He seems to have been the black sheep of the Priestley family, incapable in his earlier days of holding a job for long, and an embarrassment to his father. Eventually he too came to America, married Margaret Fulker, and did a little farming near Northumberland, Pennsylvania, where his family had moved in 1796. But trouble was brewing between parent and child, trouble that has never been fully explained but led to serious consequences. In April 1800 the local newspaper accused William of trying to poison his father by putting arsenic in the flour chest. His precise motive remains a mystery. Both father and son denied the allegation in the newspapers in June, but William had already decamped in shame. The old man was clearly upset by the attempted patricide, but he retired his

Detail of the book room, Oliver Ames Memorial Library, North Easton, Massachusetts, 1877–78. Turned and carved ornament of butternut wood executed by artisans working for O. W. Norcross, Richardson's favorite builder, adds richness to the library interior.

son's debts, and in a letter said that he felt more compassion for than resentment toward his offspring. "He is gone to seek a settlement in the Western Territory, and I do not expect, or wish to see him any more." But, he added, he would maintain contact with him and "give him my best advice." At his death, in 1804, it is said, Joseph left an annuity to his daughter-in-law Margaret Fulker Priestley, carefully drawn so that William could not touch it.

Go West, young man, especially if you hope to shuck the past and begin anew. William and Margaret left Pennsylvania in 1800 and were in Louisiana by the next year, perhaps drawn there by its French heritage, although at the moment it was nominally Spanish territory. By the time of the congressional ratification of Jefferson's Louisiana Purchase, in October 1803, the Priestleys owned a sugar plantation on the Mississippi River in St. James Parish; they added to it in 1817 and later. William and Margaret had four children, one of whom, Catherine Caroline Priestley, married Bermuda-born Henry Dickenson Richardson, probably in 1836. They in turn produced four children, of whom Henry Hobson Richardson was the oldest.

Caroline Richardson gave birth to the future architect on September 29, 1838, at her parents' place some sixty miles upriver from New Orleans. It was a fair day in the low fifties, according to the agricultural diary of the Priestleys' neighbor, the distinguished planter Valcour Aime. The Richardsons were New Orleans people, so Catherine was probably escaping the threat of the yellow fever or cholera that visited the city almost every summer during these years. The house at Priestley Plantation, on the low-lying delta land on the west bank of the

Trackside exterior of the Old Colony Railroad Depot, North Easton, Massachusetts, 1881–84. The sheltering roof, geometrical clarity, horizontal proportions, and natural materials of Richardson's work created an image that was later to influence the buildings of Frank Lloyd Wright.

Mississippi, has not survived. Priestley's narrow strip of land, however, stretched back from the river between Jacques Roman's property, which still holds the showcase antebellum house Oak Alley, and the Fortier and Aime plantations. The house at Priestley Plantation was no doubt less grand than its neighbors, but the Richardsons and their children, who regularly summered between Roman's and Aime's, would certainly have known these places well. From them we gain some insight into the summertime, river-road ambience familiar to Richardson as a boy.

The economy of antebellum southern Louisiana centered around the sugar industry, and St. James Parish was in the heart of the most-productive sugar lands in the country. In the years before and during Richardson's childhood, production expanded rapidly. His grandfather William, who died four years before his birth, does not show up in histories of the industry, and his may have been a mere cane farm, but he apparently grew financially comfortable, if not actually wealthy, from it. The Louisiana sugar country was a labyrinthine, level river land of large cane plantations interspersed with narrow sugar farms. Cane mills, sugarhouses with tall chimneys, and slave cabins dotted the landscape. In 1850 St. James Parish counted a population of 3,285 whites and 7,751 slaves. Great mansions were plentiful along the banks of the various rivers. In St. James, Oak Alley and another, called Uncle Sam, survive as the most impressive.

Carriage entrance, Old Colony Railroad Depot, North Easton, Massachusetts, 1881–84. Members of the Ames family built this depot as a point of transition from carriage to train and back again as they commuted between the commercial center of Boston and their outlying domestic retreats.

Valcour Aime Plantation, St. James Parish, Louisiana, 1830s. Richardson spent the summers of his youth on his grandmother's cane farm between this antebellum mansion and Oak Alley, a similar house on the Jacques Roman plantation.

Jacques Roman's Oak Alley was a new house at Richardson's birth. A masterpiece of Louisiana Greek Revival architecture, it sits well back from the Mississippi at the end of a vista of arching live oaks that give it its name. The two-story house rises from a square plan and is completely surrounded by colossal Doric columns supporting a gallery beneath an all-encompassing hip roof. The building is typical of the river houses of the area, and they must have impressed the young Richardson. Oak Alley and its kind were precursors of the sheltering, inclusive roof forms the architect was to use on many of his most successful buildings. And when, in 1874, he moved his family into a house in Brookline, Massachusetts, it was of that type known locally as a "Jamaican planter's house," a hip-roofed wooden block preceded by a porch sustained by colossal piers.

The famous Valcour Aime establishment, on the other side of the Priestleys', included a refinery begun in 1834. This eventually housed machinery valued at $60,000 and capable of producing very high-grade sugar. Production rose more or less annually during Richardson's youth, to a record 450,000 hogsheads in 1853. The plantation is the subject of a chapter in the reminiscences of Eliza Ripley, who, like the future architect, grew up in New Orleans in the years before the Civil War. She was an old lady when she published her memoirs, in 1912, but her recollection proves to have been sharp. Eliza was fifteen when she visited the Aime family in 1847; the younger Richardson was nine that year. In his own diary Valcour Aime interrupted his dull listing of thermometer readings and crop conditions to report that yellow fever was ravaging New Orleans that summer. Escaping from the city to the safety of the upriver plantations, Eliza rode on *La*

Belle Créole, a packet boat that leisurely plied the sluggish Mississippi waters, stopping at almost every landing to take on or discharge passengers. Deck hands held the unsteady plank as the teenager and her party were landed at Aime's, about midnight. Slaves with torches lighted the short walk to the house. The next morning she awoke to the scent of roses and café au lait.

The Valcour Aime household included the family, an army of slaves, and (as did Augustine St. Clare's Louisiana establishment in Harriet Beecher Stowe's contemporary novel *Uncle Tom's Cabin*) a governess from New England. Guests were frequent and legion. Eliza remembered a U-shaped, two-storied mansion open to the rear and facing the river. It is gone now, but photographs show that from the front it looked much like Oak Alley, with colossal Doric columns supporting an encompassing hip roof. The brick- and stone-paved ground floor contained small and grand dining rooms, the office, and various service spaces, all one-room deep and surrounding a square courtyard that was the center of domestic life. There sat "madame's basket, mademoiselle's embroidery frame, the box of cigars, and comfortable lounging chairs." It must have been arcaded because at the upper level a gallery ran around the three sides of the court, giving access to airy living and sleeping rooms. Richardson may have remembered this living arrangement when he later proposed similar outdoor living areas for suburban houses on Staten Island.

Valcour Aime's main house rested in a spacious garden, famous as Le Petit Versailles but nonetheless conceived as a *jardin anglais* by a Dijon landscape designer. The elder Eliza remembered parterres, rustic and stone bridges over tiny rivers, and vine-draped summerhouses. Most "wonderful and surprising" to her as a teenager was an octagonal pagoda with stained-glass windows and—farther on—a "mountain" from which to view *tout ensemble.*

The Aime plantation also contained a hospital, store, church, school, sugar mill, slave quarters, and other outbuildings. Other local plantations, including Duncan Keller's in St. James Parish, boasted of stables filled with fine horses. The planters loved their horseflesh. Some great plantations—as well as the city of New Orleans itself—even had their own racecourses.

It is probably safe to assume that young Henry Richardson also experienced these neighboring wonders, as well as his grandmother's holdings. Priestley Plantation lacked many of the amenities of Valcour Aime's, but it did support a sugarhouse, engine houses, and other outbuildings at the time it was sold, in 1858. And there were certainly barns to shelter the cattle and quarters to house the twenty-nine slaves working on the place in that year. Richardson spent his earliest summers in this environment, and there remained something of the plantation gentleman about him throughout his life. In his obituary of the architect, Phillips Brooks reminded his readers that it was unwise to forget Richardson's Southern origins.

Exterior of the F. L. Ames Gate Lodge, North Easton,
Massachusetts, 1880–81. Richardson combined the dominant
hipped roof of the antebellum Louisiana mansions he knew in
his youth with rugged masonry composed of local granite
boulders to create an architecture that is one with its setting,
a landscape designed by Frederick Law Olmsted.

The architect's daughter Julia Shepley says in her memoir that Richardson returned to the South to claim Priestley Plantation at his mother's death, in 1866, bringing gifts to the many ex-slaves whom he knew by name. It is a story that contradicts the facts. Caroline's mother, Margaret Fulker Priestley, had moved to New Orleans as early as 1854 and died in 1857. Priestley Plantation was sold the next year by her three surviving children to pay off her debts, and it does not seem that Richardson inherited much from his grandmother; nor did he return to Louisiana once he left.

Summer life at Priestley Plantation was, however, a sometime thing. William and Margaret's surviving children all left St. James Parish for the city during the 1830s. When he married Catherine Priestley, Henry D. Richardson's business interests centered in New Orleans, and the family spent the majority of its time there. The combination of the city's French tradition, leisure-loving ways, seaport bustle, frontier spirit, cultural diversity, and wealth made New Orleans unique among the cities of the United States. It was the antithesis of the isolated and well-scrubbed villages of New England and the Western Reserve. All this gave New Orleans the reputation as the most glamorous and decadent city in the country, but it was also the most unhealthy.

New Orleans is the product of the Mississippi. Its low-lying lands top a thousand feet of muck brought down by the great river. By the 1850s the city was known for its periodic epidemics of disease. While the antebellum period saw enormous growth—the population leaping from about 46,000 in 1830 to around 116,000 in 1850—according to the local Unitarian minister, the Reverend Theodore Clapp, these epidemics brought "uniform, unvaried, heart-sickening, and depressing gloom" during the hot months nearly every year. Yellow fever, cholera, and typhus all lurked in the poor drainage, poor water supply, and filthy streets. In the yellow fever epidemic of 1853, when the city became one "huge lazar house, the abode of dead or dying," eighty-one hundred people perished in just over four months. Although the Richardsons, like many of their class, tried to avoid the perils of disease by summering in St. James Parish, the family did not entirely escape visitations of pestilence.

The Richardsons' life was largely centered in the new American Quarter—the St. Mary suburb, or Second Municipality, beyond Canal Street. In the early years of the nineteenth century, the city spread upriver, away from the French Quarter, beginning with St. Mary, absorbing one plantation after another as faubourgs, or suburbs, added them to the colonial urban core. Older plantation houses of the type we know from St. James Parish were quickly surrounded by new streets and new houses. Richardson's father, like most of his commercial class, sought economic gain in these developing areas, and his son here too might have come to know and admire peripteral plantation architecture.

This view from the tower of St. Patrick's Church shows the Thirteen Sisters, also known as the Julia Street Row, erected between Camp and St. Charles Streets in the new suburb of St. Mary, New Orleans, 1832–33. At his birth, Richardson's family lived at No. 143, the second from the corner of St. Charles (here to the right). Parson Clapp's Gothic Unitarian church of the early 1850s appears at the lower right.

While the Richardsons were members of the comfortable mercantile slave-holding middle class, whatever wealth the Priestleys possessed did not prevent Henry D. Richardson from seeking income in a variety of endeavors. At the time of young Henry's birth, his father was speculating in real estate, buying and selling lots of uptown land and building at least one house there, buying and selling slaves, and working as a cotton broker with the firm of T. S. Hobson and Company, from which we assume the future architect derived his middle name. During the next decade the elder Richardson's situation changed significantly. He left Hobson as cotton prices in New Orleans began to decline to an all-time low, in 1845, resided through the middle of the decade in Jefferson Parish, a little farther upriver, then returned to the city, apparently to work for his wife's family's business, the Priestley and Bein Hardware Company. Henry D. Richardson may have been traveling for that company when he died in Philadelphia, in July 1854, after a "lingering illness" described in the city's death records as "abscess of liver." He was then in his mid-forties.

But at young Henry's birth, in 1838, the Richardsons lived in one of the Thirteen Buildings, or Thirteen Sisters, a new row of Federal style town houses on the upper side of Julia Street between Camp and St. Charles Streets. These are more extensive than but characteristic of the Anglo-American houses erected in the area during the 1830s. The Anglophile Julia Street row, like many other new town houses in the sector, owes its refined neoclassical appearance to the works of London's Robert Adam or Boston's Charles Bulfinch, and contrasts sharply with the older and folksier Creole architecture of the city. The entire block is a uniform series of redbrick, white-trim, three-and-a-half-story elevations with regularly spaced openings, round arched at ground level and rectangular above. The mature architect may have later recalled the partis of the river-road plantation houses, but the delicate Adamesque detail of the Julia Street row found no afterlife in his work.

Presumably young Henry moved with his family to outlying Jefferson Parish during the mid-1840s, but nothing has come to light from this interlude. The Richardsons would move back to the American Sector about the time Henry turned ten, to Carondelet Street, and perhaps to another Federal style row house of the 1830s, for they were common in the neighborhood. There he lived until he left the city.

Eliza Ripley also devotes a chapter in her memoirs to Richardson's boyhood haunts in New Orleans, for it was her neighborhood too. *La Belle Créole* landed in the vicinity for the convenience of shoppers from the upriver plantations who visited the area's wholesale houses and retail stores. The area abounded in churches of various denominations. Roman Catholic St. Patrick's, a Gothic concoction begun in the year of Richardson's birth, stands on Camp Street just around the corner from the Julia Street row. Although for Eliza religious life centered on Dr. William Leacock's Episcopal Christ Church at Canal and Baronne Streets, the Richardsons, given Caroline's descent from Dr. Priestley, favored Theodore Clapp's Congregational Unitarian Church of the Messiah. New Orleans had from early in the century a markedly latitudinarian viewpoint in religious matters, as represented by the denominational mix in Richardson's neighborhood. It was an attitude that seems to have rubbed off on him.

Parson Clapp's church began life in the 1830s as the plain brick First Congregational Church at St. Charles and Gravier Streets, just four blocks from Julia Street. Among its incorporators in 1833 was John D. Bein, family business associate and H. H. Richardson's future stepfather. After a fire in 1851, a new church, octagonal and Gothic, rose on the "downtown-river" corner (that toward the old quarter and the river) of St. Charles and Julia Streets, a site just across from the Richardsons' first residence and still not far from their current one. Among the trustees elected at the time of the rebuilding were Henry D. Richardson and John D. Bein. The minister, Massachusetts-born and Yale-educated Parson Clapp, was a devotee of liberal Unitarianism and, contradictorily but expediently, of slavery. His support came from the planter-merchant community of the American Sector.

During the 1830s and 1840s the American Sector was a bustling place. It witnessed much physical change after its administrative separation, in 1836, from the older, French section of the city. As residents of the Second Municipality, its American citizens could spend their taxes and transact business their own way, unimpeded by older, French legislation. St. Mary saw some of the city's most impressive public and private buildings erected during this period, such as theaters, hotels, exchanges, hospitals, schools, and municipal buildings. Civic improvements embraced street paving, gas lighting, and the erection of public buildings, including an imposing market house on Poydras Street and James Gallier's dignified Municipal Hall, facing Lafayette Square. All this activity within a short walk from his Julia and Carondelet Street houses must have delighted young Henry. (Kibitzing construction is still a young man's delight.) His later interest in the granite buildings of midcentury Boston may have stemmed from their Southern cousins, for New Orleans in this period was lining its streets with commercial and civic monuments partly of granite, all influenced by Boston. The Cammack Stores, erected in 1851 in Richardson's neighborhood at Carondelet and Common Streets, like many other local examples, had a first floor of the granite post-and-lintel construction common in Massachusetts.

In fact, the granite was itself imported from New England. As early as 1825 Germain Musson (who was, incidentally, the grandfather of the artist Edgar Degas) erected at Canal and Royal Streets a series of buildings with post-and-lintel storefronts and rough-faced Quincy granite upper walls, buildings as up-to-date as anything in Boston. The stone came down the coast in ships that hauled Musson's cotton on the return journey to New England.

All this construction must have caught young Richardson's eye, but a boy's attention span can be brief. Eliza Ripley recalled other street scenes that attracted her as a child, the sorts of things likely to have captured Henry's interest as well: flocks of turkeys, for example, that were marched up Camp Street at holiday time to be sold "on the hoof" and served roasted or broiled with oyster dressing. In this lowland the streets were often flooded after a rain; snakes, frogs, and crawfish abounded in the adjacent swamps. "Fine fishing place for us little ones it was," she remembered.

Eliza also remembered the inhabitants of the Julia Street row. During the early 1840s these impressive homes were occupied "by the leading social element of the American colony." These were the professional and mercantile leaders of the young American community: the Lanfears, the Slocombs, the Urquharts, the Branders, the Smiths, the Buckners, and the Mathewses, as well as—at least briefly—the Richardsons and Eliza's own family. If young Richardson had contact with any of these people, he was in useful company indeed. In his maturity he aspired to a place in the Boston equivalent of such fashionable society.

Young Richardson, or Fez, as he was called by his family and friends even beyond his college years, lived with his parents and eventually three siblings: a brother, William, and two sisters, Catherine (Kitty) and Margaret. His father, twenty-nine at young Richardson's birth, died about the time Fez turned sixteen. The loss must have sorely tried the teenager, but he was not to remain fatherless for long; two years later, in 1856, Catherine Priestley Richardson married John

Davey Bein. A Scottish-born fifty-two-year-old who had long been a friend and business associate of the Priestley and Richardson families, John Bein had lost his first wife to cholera just a few months after the death of Henry D. Richardson. Caroline's brother William Priestley Jr., who perished in the yellow fever epidemic of 1841, and the rest of the Priestleys had invested with Bein in the hardware business; the elder Richardson had been associated with the same concern. The firm of Priestley and Bein purveyed a full line of hardware items, including Pennsylvania iron bars and boilerplate and Oliver Ames shovels, made in North Easton, Massachusetts, a company town the architect would eventually enhance with a number of his finest buildings.

After the Civil War the architect's sister Kitty was to marry John W. Labouisse, another Julia Street name; William married Mary Scudday; and Margaret, Henry Leverich. The four Richardson children in their own right were to produce twenty-five offspring, a number of whom became architects and went on to sire an astonishing number of other architects, to the fourth and fifth (the present) generations.

Little information reaches us about Richardson's early upbringing. Certainly he and his family lived a life of some comfort in Julia and later Carondelet Street. Modern biography seems to demand strife between parent and child, but there is little reason to suspect that the Richardsons' home life was anything but congenial. We know almost nothing of his relationship to his father, but there seems to have been some warmth between him and his stepfather, whom he must have known all his young life. During the occupation of New Orleans in the 1860s, Richardson expressed genuine concern for his mother and sisters, and he was sad when his mother died just after his return from Paris following the war. A slight shadow is thrown by his never returning to New Orleans once he left the city, but there was no break in communication, and his openness and optimism as an adult seem strong evidence for an untroubled childhood.

Not until a short time before his father's death, in 1854, do we have definite notice of young Fez. In that—his fifteenth—year, he applied, or rather his father applied on his behalf, for admission to the military academy at West Point. This generated letters of recommendation, one from his father and one from his teacher George Blackman, to Jefferson Davis, then secretary of war for the United States. These letters describe an attractive and accomplished teenager, but what letter of recommendation written by such advocates would not? From them we learn that at the age of nine Richardson entered a private classical academy, run by Blackman not far from the Richardson house, and had been in attendance ever since

Exterior of the Hayden Building, Boston, 1875. The upper floors of this building recall the stonework of the Granite style Richardson knew in New Orleans as a child and in Boston as an undergraduate.

H. H. Richardson, ca. 1852. The earliest known likeness of the future architect, this photograph was taken in New Orleans during his early teens.

with the exception of parts of the year, when, presumably, he summered at Priestley Plantation. Not once had young Henry's deportment or application required "physical coercion," we learn. He neither lied nor cursed, and he was above the average in mental capacity. For a boy of his age he was a fair Latin scholar, having read Cornelius Nepos (probably his *De Viris Illustribus*), Caesar, and Virgil; he had commenced Greek and had acquired a good general knowledge of geography and history.

In mathematics he was the most promising student George Blackman had ever taught. He had finished the third, or advanced, part of Frederick Emerson's *North American Arithmetic*, Charles Davies's *Elementary Algebra*, the early parts of Davies's adaptation of Louis-Pierre-Marie Bourdon's *Elements of Algebra*, and Davies's adaptation of A. M. Legendre's *Elementary Geometry and Trigonometry*. These were all standard texts, available in several recent editions. He had a "good knowledge" of French, according to his father, and could speak it with "tolerable facility." There must be some exaggeration here about his abilities both as a mathematician and a linguist, for Richardson later found it necessary to retake the entrance examination at the École des Beaux-Arts in Paris—an exam given in French, of course —because of a weakness in geometry.

To the information in these documents can be added secondary data given by the critic Mariana Van Rensselaer, Richardson's first biographer, who had known him and who wrote when many of the architect's friends and family were alive to supply her with reminiscences. She reports a "merry boy," a good preparatory student, an excellent athlete, a good horseman, and, like his father, an expert at fencing. We are even told that he was a skilled chess player, so skilled in fact that he could play several games at once, blindfolded. Music, too, attracted him, and he played the flute. Horsemanship and flute playing, we remember, had been accomplishments of Dr. Priestley, and a love of horses was characteristic of the planter society of the river road. This list of youthful accomplishments smacks of posthumous praise for a great man, but if only half of it is true, Richardson was a gifted lad indeed.

George Blackman wrote that he knew of no physical defect that would disqualify young Richardson from the military academy. Here, as we shall see, he might have been dissembling. The lad had a sound constitution and enjoyed good health. He stood five feet tall, according to his father, rather stumpy for a fifteen-year-old. If this is accurate, he must have gotten a spurt of late growth to have achieved a stature even approaching six feet in his maturity. Blackman noted a finely formed head, dark hair and eyes, and spirited expression. Although all other descriptions of Richardson stress his pleasant nature, here he is said to have possessed a "nervous bilious temperament." He was also ambitious of distinction, eager to please, "steady and persevering in the pursuit of an object." His teacher thought him surpassed by few boys his age in generosity and courage. Finally, Blackman had no doubt that, if admitted to the Point, Richardson would do credit to himself and honor to his country.

Despite these endorsements and that of Louisiana senator Judah P. Benjamin, who raised and refined sugar on his own plantation below New Orleans, H. H. Richardson was not admitted to the military academy. He would be prepared for neither the Union nor the Confederate army in the ensuing war. We do not know why he was turned down. Perhaps, as Mariana Van Rensselaer reported, it was his speech impediment, despite Blackman's assertion that he had no physical defect that might disqualify him. Indeed, later in life it was said that his speech came out like a series of explosions. The admissions office at West Point, however, probably had no information about his stammer. It would have known only what it read in his application papers. In any event, Richardson spent the following months at the University of Louisiana, around the corner from his home. There, it is said, he continued to excel in mathematics, but he left to attend Harvard College in the late summer of 1855.

Once turned toward the Northeast, he did not look back. There were moments during the Civil War when he thought he ought to be in New Orleans with his family, but then and later it was obvious to all—to his mother, his fiancée, his friend Henry Adams, and others—that however much his Southern upbringing had shaped his basic personality, his future lay in the North. He left Louisiana as a teenager; the final molding of his character and the laying of the foundation of his career would take place in Cambridge, Massachusetts.

SEVER HALL

3 ❖ CAMBRIDGE 1855–59

CAMBRIDGE MADE THE MAN. IT MUST HAVE BEEN SOMETIME AROUND his seventeenth birthday when H. H. Richardson arrived in Massachusetts. Economic and cultural ties between the American Sector of New Orleans and Anglo-Saxon New England had always been close. Commerce by sea carried cotton and other staples north, granite and manufactured articles south. Priestley and Bein sold Massachusetts shovels, we remember, and many a prominent citizen of the Crescent City, like Unitarian Parson Clapp, stemmed from the Northeast. The lines of communication remained strong, even in a time of threatening division. This was especially true in Cambridge.

The Harvard College class of 1859, Richardson's class, counted six students from below the Mason-Dixon line among its ninety-nine members. Southerners had begun to invade this center of New England ideals as early as the eighteenth century, and they continued to arrive in surprisingly large numbers in the middle of the nineteenth, despite rising sectional tensions. Harvard between 1855 and 1861 admitted sixty-seven of them out of a total enrollment of 623. The great majority stemmed from Baltimore and New Orleans. They came from wealthy and powerful families and gave to the college something of its reputation as a nursery for aristocrats.

For the most part little tension existed among the students in these antebellum years. Although Henry Adams (class of 1858) did recall much later that Northerners and Southerners well knew "how an edge separated them in 1856 from mortal enmity," the college formed, in the words of another of its students, "a little world by itself" where a sea of camaraderie washed away sectional strife. The nearly daily entries from 1856–58 in the private journal of Adams's classmate Benjamin Crowninshield of Boston only once mention the word "abolition." This appears when he describes a visit to Boston with some friends to hear the "Slave Singers." They found they had stumbled into an abolitionist meeting and did not stay. In frequent references to Richardson, Crowninshield never mentions his origins. The sons of slaveholding Southerners, like Richardson, must have felt somewhat stressed by abolitionist Boston, but we hear nothing of that from him or his Harvard peers.

Harvard when Richardson matriculated had physically evolved over its more than two centuries into a core series of redbrick Georgian and Federal buildings

OPPOSITE: *Detail of the east elevation, Sever Hall, Harvard University, Cambridge, Massachusetts, 1878–80. Sunlight plays delightfully across the cut, carved, and molded brick forms of Richardson's contribution to the architecture of Harvard Yard.*

Front entrance of the F. L. Ames Gate Lodge, North Easton, Massachusetts, 1880–81. Richardson may have studied the emerging science of geology with Louis Agassiz at Harvard, for some of his later buildings are characterized by the use of granite stones shaped by glacial, Ice Age forces first explained by the scientist.

along the east side of Peabody Street north of Massachusetts Avenue. He would have felt architecturally right at home, with the college vaguely reminding his untrained eye of buildings like the Julia Street row of his early days. Charles Bulfinch's gray granite University Hall across Harvard Yard had also been in service for a generation, and it too may have looked somewhat familiar to him from the work rising in his boyhood neighborhood. The newest building on campus, a ten-year-old library named Gore Hall, designed by Bostonian Richard Bond, was a romantic Gothic Revival confection whose paired towers and pointed windows made it look like a church. Perhaps the new student barely noticed any of this or had only the general curiosity of the usual sidewalk observer, developed from days of watching new construction during his childhood, for he had not yet decided on a career in architecture.

To enter Harvard in the 1850s, a prospect had to pass a grueling two-day series of written and oral examinations given in University Hall. On the first day, after breakfast, he answered in arithmetic and Latin and Greek grammar, followed by history. The session ended with a three-hour exam in Latin, Greek,

Bridge in the Back Bay Fens, Boston, 1880–84. Richardson punctuated F. L. Olmsted's rolling tract of land and water with this flowing and leaping ashlar span.

algebra, and geometry. One student later tagged this the hardest day of his life and as "disagreeable" as any he remembered. On the second day the aspirant sat for exams in Cicero, Felton's Greek reader, Latin prosody, Virgil, and Greek poetry. If he survived this gauntlet he became a student, after posting a $400 bond with sureties to pay for all his charges.

Despite his years of studying Latin and Greek at George Blackman's academy in New Orleans, when he arrived in Cambridge Richardson needed remedial work. He bought a copy of Homer's *Odyssey* at William Ticknor's well-stocked bookshop in downtown Boston on October 6, 1855, and began to cram for entrance to Harvard in a preparatory school run by Reginald and Thomas Chase. Along with six others, Richardson gained admission to the freshman class in February of the next year, but he still required extra study of the *Agamemnon* and probably other works during the following summer and fall.

The Harvard College Richardson entered differed greatly from the internationally respected educational institution it has become. Despite its national constituency, its roots were largely provincial. According to Henry Adams, the Unitarian clergy had by his day stamped "a character of moderation, balance, judgment, [and] restraint" on the institution. "As far as it educated at all," he wrote in his famous book *The Education of Henry Adams*, it was a "mild and liberal school" that taught very little, and that little badly, but "left the mind open, free from bias, ignorant of facts, but docile." Adams's biographer Ernest Samuels has observed that this was a somewhat twisted memory, that Adams in fact laid the foundation of his intellectual life at the college. Adams's assessment was not all negative, however, for he also wrote that even if a graduate did not know much, "his mind remained supple, ready to receive knowledge." And, if nothing else,

Harvard instilled in its students a calm self-assurance that taught them to stand on their own two feet. In some that produced snobbishness; in Richardson it produced an independence of mind.

The venerable old college had struck bottom in the 1850s, according to its eminent historian Samuel Eliot Morison. Arthritic Rev. James Walker held the presidency, one of a series of good men and able scholars who proved to be managerial misfits during these years. Student unruliness was the rule, pranks were common, disturbances in the yard a nightly occurrence. Although the need for curricular reform came under discussion during Richardson's Harvard days, little changed other than that oral finals replaced written. The classics remained as they had always been: basic and required. Learning proceeded by rote; courses involved daily recitation and bone-numbing repetition in large classes. The words of Josiah Quincy, president of Harvard until 1845, that students "got their lessons" by graded daily recitation and discipline, still held sway, especially among the older faculty. Grading resulted from a complex system of points and demerits under the jurisdiction of a Parietal Committee, which created the climate of a police state. The intellectual atmosphere had a limiting and stultifying impact, and Richardson, who possessed uncommon and inventive intelligence, at first barely managed to survive it.

Intellectual life at Harvard was regimented. No electives existed for the lower classes, so as a freshman Richardson must have taken Greek, Latin, mathematics, history, rhetoric, French, natural history, and chemistry. Taught by constant drills and quizzes, these classes lasted for seven hours after compulsory morning prayers, to which students were summoned by the college bell at seven. Only in his senior year did Richardson have some choice. After the required philosophy, rhetoric, and physics, he could have elected to study modern languages, modern literature, anatomy, or geology.

No record survives of what subjects Richardson did study. Perhaps he joined Henry Adams, Benjamin Crowninshield, and others at the scientific lectures of Louis Agassiz, father of glacial theory and a teacher of "infectious enthusiasm." Adams remembered Agassiz's talks on the Glacial Period as the "only teaching that appealed to his imagination." There exists, alas, no record of any special interest in the sciences on the part of Richardson, this undergraduate descendant of Dr. Priestley. And yet, as we shall see, some of his later works depend heavily upon a familiarity with, if not exact knowledge of, the earth sciences evolving during his lifetime. These works would be shaped as geological analogies inspired by and emerging from the glacial landscape of New England.

In college Richardson read not only for course work. Far from it. He labored through the classics, but then as later he also read modern history and fiction. While he borrowed no books from the college library in Gore Hall (and there is preserved a ledger that says who did), he bought a range of titles at Ticknor's

during his first year in town. They included not only histories, such as Prescott's *Reign of Philip II* and Macauley's *England*—standard fare for any person aspiring to be educated in that period—but popular British literature such as Sir Walter Scott's Waverley novels, Charles Lever's *Charles O'Malley, the Irish Dragoon*, and Henry Cockton's *Valentine Vox, the Ventriloquist*. Richardson may have already known his Waverley, for Mark Twain makes it evident in *Life on the Mississippi* that the Scotsman's tales were well known in Louisiana in the architect's youth. Scott, Twain wrote, ran "the people mad . . . with his medieval romances." As an

Exterior of the Robert Treat Paine house, Waltham, Massachusetts, 1884–87. The forms of nature and forms created by man play off one another in the rough-stone tower and archway and the geometrical precision and Palladian upper window of this dramatic gable end.

East front of Sever Hall, Harvard University, Cambridge, Massachusetts, 1878–80. The architect chose a restricted vocabulary of traditional materials, then manipulated them so that the exterior would be enlivened by contrasts of bulge and flat, window and wall, light and shadow.

architect Richardson would lean heavily upon the Middle Ages.

Animated and droll scenes by Phiz, Dickens's favorite illustrator, enlivened *Charles O'Malley*, Charles Lever's rollicking picaresque novel about a lovable Irish rogue. Henry Cockton's popular *Valentine Vox*, with many comic engravings by Thomas Onwhyn in the manner of George Cruikshank, is humorous, farcical, and mischievous. In the following years Richardson's reading became more elevated. He bought and presumably read the poetry of Robert Burns and William Wordsworth. And he paid $24 for a collection of engravings after the paintings of David Wilkie, a British follower of the Dutch genre tradition.

Like many another Southerner, young Richardson achieved a less than distinguished academic record at college. Fellow Harvardian Phillips Brooks, later to be his primary client at Trinity Church, wrote an obituary in which he remembered Richardson's undergraduate period as "days of carelessness and plenty." He seemed less serious about life than even the average student, according to Brooks, who recalled only Richardson's interest in mathematics. Even there, however, he did not rank at the top of his class. Nor were his extracurricular activities always acceptable, and a student's standing was established by a combination of academic success and approved deportment. The regimentation triggered occasional revolt; even Henry Adams met frequent chastisement. On at least one occasion in his sophomore year, Richardson received demerits for creating a noisy disturbance in Harvard Yard. And he set records for cutting recitations and avoiding obligatory religious services. Between January and June of his senior year, Richardson skipped chapel forty times. The college's compulsory religious exercises—every morning, evening, and on Sundays, when all-day preaching was not infrequent—probably dampened whatever religious enthusiasm Richardson might have brought to Cambridge. He would never be churchgoing, despite his Unitarian background and the fact that many of his friends, like the Right Reverend Brooks, became men of the cloth. Like that of many another lusterless undergraduate, Richardson's career proves that success in life does not always depend upon toeing the mark or early academic achievement.

In Henry Adams's view, a Southerner in general "had no mind; he had temperament." He was not a scholar as a rule, but, Adams added, in life one could get along without ideas "if one had only the social instinct." Richardson proved a partial exception to Adams's rule, for he eventually became capable of both

West front of Sever Hall, Harvard University, Cambridge, Massachusetts, 1878–80. Simplicity of silhouette matches a restricted palette of materials to create a quiet architecture.

serious—if not scholarly—work and congenial play. But during his early years at Harvard he devoted himself largely to play. Academics could take care of themselves. When he arrived at college, Richardson's dark handsomeness and athletic body gave no promise of the bloated figure familiar from his later days. His presence, his personal charm, his family pedigree, and his ready cash greased his entrance into the undergraduate society of Harvard. He was clubbable. Without his Harvard social connections he would have had no architectural practice, or at least a very different one. As the years unfolded, Richardson's professional and social life transpired largely within the circle of old school ties.

Harvard's regimented academic life did not preclude a social side. The activities ticked off by Benjamin Crowninshield in his journal seem neatly balanced between study and recitation, on the one hand, and convivial gatherings, either at college or in Boston, on the another (not to mention the killing of a snake in the yard and, after a "considerable fight" and with Richardson's help, of a bat in his Hollis Hall room). The diarist played cards frequently, including whist with Richardson and others. The students often walked or took the car into the city, where Bacon & Ripley's billiard hall in Temple Place appears to have been the point of common gathering. There were more-elevated destinations as well, including the Athenaeum to view works of art, or the Boston Museum and other theaters for the latest in dramatic entertainment. In September 1857 Crowninshield and Fez (as he is still called in the journal) went to see one of the Booth brothers in *Hamlet*; early the next year the diarist ran into Richardson at an afternoon concert at the Music Hall.

The Southerners as a group ranked high socially and poor academically. Undergraduate life can provide scholarship or comradeship or both; for Richardson, comradeship seems easily to have gained the upper hand. Brooks recalled that he was known "only for the peculiar charm of his bright, open nature and for the sunshine which he brought into every company he entered." He had money to burn and friendships to make, and Henry Adams, who graduated a year ahead of Richardson, noted his progress. Stuffily secure in his distinguished New England heritage, the grandson and great-grandson of presidents, Adams remembered his fellow Harvardian as coming from beyond the pale, and socially on the make. "A student like H. H. Richardson," he later wrote, "who came from far away New Orleans, and had his career before him to chase rather than to guide, might make valuable friendships at college"—as indeed he did, through membership in campus social clubs such as the Hasty Pudding, to which he was initiated in October 1857, the Porcellian, which formally embraced him in April 1858, and the Pierian Sodality. The foundations of the Porcellian were laid, according to a nineteenth-century description, upon sociability, brotherly affection, and generosity, as well as liberality, courtesy, and the "spirit of a true Gentleman." Nothing here concerning scholarship.

Stone deaf President Walker and his faculty added music to the elective curriculum in 1856. We know most about undergraduate Richardson in connection with his own musical interests. As member of the Pierian Sodality, the campus musical club, he played second flute, and in his sophomore year he helped revive a struggling organization devoted to the promotion of "musical study and skill." Not only music occupied the Pierians, however. Richardson was initiated into the sodality in March 1857, and on the occasion he was expected to provide the club's entertainment. After "somewhat brief and *decidedly informal*" proceedings in the secretary's rooms, the company retired for a jolly time at Boston's famed hostelry the Parker house. There Richardson hosted a "spread" that Crowninshield thought "generous" and the official records of the organization judged the best ever. And how could it have been otherwise, "with so notorious a connoisseur as Mr. R. to do the polite?" His generous hospitality had long ago labeled him as "a jolly good fellow." The evening abounded "in everything that the most fastidious Pierian could ask," with throats "unsparingly moistened with Parker's choicest brand of wine."

The celebration at Parker's lasted late, and the woozy Pierians had to hurry as best they could to catch the last car for Cambridge. This seems to have been a common occurrence—undergraduates drank too much then as now. Crowninshield's diary is riddled with what he euphemized as "salubrious" or "breezy" episodes; it contains more than one reference to vomiting on the floor of his room or being so hung over as to be nearly incapacitated. When as an old man Henry Adams wrote his autobiography, he marveled at the students' "habit of drinking —though the mere recollection of it made him doubt his own veracity, so fantastic it seemed later in life." Richardson was neither the first nor the last underclassman to cut loose when he got to college, nor will this be the last time we encounter him raising a glass at the head of a groaning table surrounded by appreciative friends.

Appreciative friends equal potential clients. Although Richardson, this early —he was just eighteen at the time—probably had no serious thought of his future career, consciously or unconsciously he was creating a network of college friends who would hire his services in the years to come. James A. Rumrill, secretary of the Pierian Sodality and chronicler of the evening at Parker's, was to influence the choice of architect for Richardson's first job, the Church of the Unity in Springfield, Massachusetts, and as a railroad executive would throw other business his way throughout his career. Some of the other college mates for whom he later worked were Benjamin Crowninshield, who seems to have been the treasurer of all of Richardson's clubs, Phillips Brooks, Nicholas L. Anderson, Henry Adams, and Frederick L. Ames. These men provided him with opportunities to create some of his most important buildings. Although Edward W. "Ned" Hooper never hired the architect to design for him personally, as treasurer of Harvard College

South front of Austin Hall, Harvard University, Cambridge, Massachusetts, 1880–84. A living donor (such as Edward Austin) could be cajoled into increasing his gift as the work unfolded, so this building is the more elaborate of the two Richardson designed for Harvard.

in the 1870s and 1880s he commissioned both Sever and Austin Halls for their alma mater. And he was Richardson's landlord during his Brookline years.

David Hyslop "Hyte" Hayden of Boston, another Pierian who played billiards at Ripley's in Boston, also graduated with Richardson's class. He never commissioned work from the architect, but he did introduce his classmate to his sister Julia. Rumrill recorded the moment when the Pierians became aware of brother Richardson's interest in women. On the evening of May 4, 1857, at the end of his sophomore year, he left a grand party in the sodality's rooms in remarkable shape—that is, "in a state of *perfect sobriety.*" The group had scheduled its first public performance the next day, but that had not turned Richardson so suddenly—although not permanently—into a teetotaler. According to the secretary it was the result of *"feminine influence."* Under that influence Richardson exhibited "moral courage & self denial" to a degree that, Rumrill thought, would be remembered, admired, and respected by future Pierians. In late May 1858, Crowninshield ran into Fez and "Miss Julia" at the Athenaeum, looking at the pictures, and by the middle of his senior year, in February 1859, Richardson was engaged. But Julia Hayden had a very long wait before becoming his wife.

Social distraction seems to have led Richardson to forget the folks at home. In June 1856 he had received permission to return to New Orleans before the end of term. No record says he went South, and he had not otherwise kept in close contact with Louisiana. On the very day of the premier performance of the Pierians, May 5, 1857, Richardson's new stepfather, John D. Bein, sat down in New Orleans to write a letter to Harvard's president, James Walker. On behalf of his mother, Bein asked for news of Richardson. He had not written her since the end of January. How were his studies and his behavior? Questions arose because he had lately "been much too lavish with the money that has been remitted to him." Bein innocently mentioned that of course his mother did not for a moment think that he gambled or drank, and so she was at a loss to explain his spending "a great deal too much money." Perhaps his "great extravagance in dress was one of the causes," and "horses is another." The stepfather then asked President Walker to give Richardson a good lecture to shame him for neglecting his mother, who had never refused him anything he had asked for. He was setting a bad example for his younger brother, William, then in Taunton, Massachusetts, preparing to enter the college.

Detail of the entrance arcade, Austin Hall, Harvard University, Cambridge, Massachusetts, 1880–84. The granite geometric patterns and the carved capitals and arches, all inspired by the Romanesque architecture of the Auvergne, establish a surface richness that is characteristic of the architect's work.

Horses did indeed race in North Cambridge near the site of present-day Porter Square, but nothing confirms that Richardson bet on the ponies, even if he did know of the sport's attractions from his boyhood in plantation country. He was, however, quite a clothes horse. His undergraduate nickname was the facetious "Nothing to Wear," probably taken from a humorous poem published during his undergraduate years. The concern for dress Richardson exhibited at college characterized him throughout life—indeed, he died in debt to, among many others, his fashionable London tailor.

We can envision the fashionable undergraduate of Richardson's years in a series of illustrations of Harvard student life drawn by Winslow Homer. Homer was then at the beginning of his career as illustrator for *Harper's Weekly;* he would eventually become one of the foremost artists of Richardson's generation. In August 1857 the magazine published his views of the annual soccer game on Cambridge Common between the Harvard freshmen and sophomores, as well as a vignette of each of the four classes. Homer was a townie, living in Cambridge but not attending the college, and this may have colored his rather unkind characterizations of Harvard undergraduates as supercilious, clubby, languid, and pampered. Or perhaps they accurately represented Richardson and his mates; Homer's views certainly would not be out of place as illustrations to Benjamin Crowninshield's journal.

Homer's individual characterizations of the classes begin with the freshmen, who seem serious enough as they study by candlelight for tomorrow's recitations. The sophomores form a rowdy group, arguing, gambling, drinking, and fencing. The juniors, and this would have been Richardson's class, passively smoke long-stemmed pipes before a roaring fire, with books abandoned at their feet. The haughty seniors, some wearing mortarboards in anticipation of graduation, read, smoke, and discuss, perhaps, what life offers them now. All of the vignettes take place in student rooms; no actual instruction appears in Homer's Harvard. His images preserve the social side, young Richardson's chosen side, of the undergraduate experience.

But just about this time Richardson may have begun to grow up. The difference Homer noticed between rowdy sophomores and contemplative juniors may have reflected Richardson's own development, for sometime late in his college career he did begin to think of his future. There was Julia, and there was the problem of a profession. Although he apparently came to Cambridge intending to draw upon his mathematical training to become an engineer, he ultimately decided on a career in architecture. While we do not know why, it seems reasonable to assume that he became interested in the profession by watching new buildings rising in Boston and at Harvard. And some of the most characteristic of them were designed by an architect he must have known personally.

Architecture in Boston during the first half of the nineteenth century was marked by the use of a local stone called Quincy granite, which is gray and tough. The Boston Granite style, as it was called even in its own day, evolved from the cool Greek Revival of early in the century to the richer-looking buildings of midcentury. In its early form it spread well beyond Boston. If Richardson had paid any attention to the new buildings rising around him during his youth in New Orleans, he would have known the basic material of the style, for works in his own neighborhood incorporated the straightforward granite block construction characteristic of the Boston building. The material itself drifted down the coast from Massachusetts. The granite established a module in the designs and a stringent look to the buildings. It was too tough to work into ornamental patterns.

A major Boston landmark of the midcentury mode, the Beacon Hill Reservoir, rose in the late 1840s behind Bulfinch's Massachusetts State house. To hold the water newly introduced into the center of town, its unknown designer created a monumental and austere basin of rough-faced granite blocks, "unvexed by details and unbroken save by a simple order of round arches," according to one nineteenth-century observer. Also in Boston, Gridley J. F. Bryant and his firm during the 1840s and 1850s designed a group of granite warehouses along the harbor. They were sturdy, severe, restrained, and simple buildings that relied for their architectural effect on crisply dressed stonework, proportions, the relationship between solid and void, and the play of textures between smoothly dressed and rough-faced stonework. Richardson later in life expressed his admiration for these buildings to the critic Montgomery Schuyler.

These were utilitarian works, but young Richardson knew of the use of this stringent Granite style in buildings of more elevated purpose, such as Edward Cabot's Boston Athenaeum, a proprietary library, or Hammatt Billings's Boston Museum, which housed both exhibitions and a theater. The museum presented the more severe version of the Athenaeum's Renaissance Revival facade. A flat stone cliff with round-arched openings facing Tremont Street, it was historically to connect the Granite style of the early century with Richardson's mature commercial work of the 1880s.

All of these Boston works exhibited a kinship with the new buildings rising at Harvard from the designs of Paul Schulze, a thirty-year-old German-born Boston architect whose musical interests brought him into contact with the Picrian Sodality. Judging from Crowninshield's many references to him, he served as the group's director or advisor, and either the club's secretary, James Rumrill, or the

Winslow Homer, "Juniors." This is a journalistic characterization of Richardson's Harvard College milieu. (Harper's Weekly, August 1, 1857)

Beacon Hill Reservoir, Boston, 1848. Mid-century Boston Granite style structures such as this greatly influenced Richardson's mature architecture.

diarist frequently visited him in his downtown office. There can be no doubt that he was well known to the Pierian's second flautist as well.

Schulze created buildings in a round-arched manner that in his native land was called the *Rundbogenstil*. It was classicizing, or Italianate, relying for the most part on simple stone masses and a minimum of applied ornament. His Appleton Chapel, under construction during Richardson's first year at college, was built of sandstone with rounded openings and an asymmetrical tower. The chapel has never been considered a successful work, and Richardson the musician must have deplored its faulty acoustics. Boylston Hall, however, erected the following year to house scientific laboratories and museums, was—and remains, even through a series of alterations—a fine example of midcentury Boston Granite style building. Nor did the Pierians fail to appreciate its quality, for Crowninshield, whose analytical chemistry class met there during his senior year, not only records a visit he made to inspect and admire the building when it was new but also put it on the tour of the yard when outside friends came to call. In Schulze's Harvard buildings, in downtown Boston, or along the city's wharves, Richardson might have seen some of the finest, quietest, and most massive lithic architecture in America. And "quiet," "massive," and "lithic" are adjectives applicable to the best of his own mature works.

At the beginning of Richardson's last semester, his stepfather wrote another letter to the college, this one addressed directly to him and carrying generous tidings. John D. Bein's long proprietorship of the Priestley and Bein Hardware Company undoubtedly meant that he had made the acquaintance of many a man in the building business. In his letter he explained that he had asked around New Orleans and been assured that an industrious architect would have a successful career in the Crescent City. Since Bein began his letter, as we all so often do, by asking pardon of his correspondent for the great length of time since he last wrote, we might assume that Richardson had begun thinking about such a career at least by the fall of 1858. But before the Civil War no school existed in the United States where a young man could prepare for such a career. While architects in this country most often graduated from the building trades or apprenticed to older men, academic training, even if it required going abroad, was the coming path into the maturing profession. Bein had in mind six or nine months in the schools of London or Paris, where Richardson might learn how to draw. He and his advisors thought that such an education would prove more rewarding than additional time spent as an apprentice in New Orleans. Bein worried somewhat about Richardson's mother's reaction to all this, but he thought she would encourage the move rather than frown upon it.

This letter addressed a different Richardson from the thoughtless sophomore lavishly spending money to entertain his chums down at Parker's. John Bein offered to make it possible for his stepson to depart for Europe at the end of his last semester in Cambridge. He aimed to give Catherine's son the education his father would have given him had he lived. As he confided to Richardson, this was in spite of the fact that he had struggled in business for the past two years and had lost a lot of money, perhaps as a result of the depression of 1857. Regarding his stepson's former spendthrift record, however, he remained touchingly optimistic. A person could live in London or Paris at very moderate expense, or he could spend a fortune, Bein told him, but "I have too good an opinion of you to think that you would abuse the confidence I put in you." He knew Richardson's aim would be to study, to advance, and not to spend money recklessly. John Bein thus made it initially possible for the aimless undergraduate to focus upon his future, to develop into a skilled architect.

If Bein here acted on knowledge rather than blind hope, Richardson must have matured from his earlier, irresponsible days. His deportment in Paris would prove this to be a correct assessment. As Henry Adams had said, Harvard instilled a sense of self-possession; whatever else it did, it "taught men to stand alone." In Cambridge, Richardson had indeed become a man.

H. H. Richardson, 1859. The future architect at the time of his graduation from Harvard College.

4 ❖ PARIS 1859–65

PARIS MADE THE ARCHITECT. RICHARDSON AND EIGHTY-NINE OTHER students received undergraduate degrees from Harvard College in July 1859. He then set out for overseas with two of his classmates, Frederic Sears Grand d'Hautville and James A. Rumrill. They crossed the North Atlantic and traveled through England, Scotland, and Ireland. Perhaps Richardson looked into the Architectural Association in London as a possible place to study (and discovered they were not ready to provide instruction to outsiders); perhaps he decided his knowledge of French and mathematics would serve him better across the channel. By mid-September, just short of his twenty-first birthday, he had a room on the Left Bank, at a pension at 41, rue de Vaugirard, near the Luxembourg Palace and within easy walking distance of the École des Beaux-Arts. John Bein had contemplated six to nine months of preparatory study abroad; with one relatively brief interlude, his stepson spent the next six years in Paris.

France was then in the midst of the Second Empire, under a government headed by Napoleon III. Between 1852 and 1870, Baron Georges-Eugène Haussmann carried out the sweeping transformation of medieval Paris ordered by the emperor. Twisted streets, picturesque vistas, and obsolete housing all vanished in the campaign. From this monumental undertaking arose the modern city, with new buildings; fresh water brought into the center through long-distance aqueducts; sewers; vast boulevards; the leveling, paving, and illuminating of streets; and new squares, parks, and public architecture. Recent and rising monuments included the New (expanded and renovated) Louvre, the Opéra, the Palais de Justice, the Church of Saint-Augustin, several theaters, and rows and rows of uniform apartment blocks lining the freshly opened streets.

Not all observers thought well of the change; some were dislocated by it. The diarist Edmond de Goncourt in 1860 lamented the vanishing of his Paris. He thought of himself as a stranger "to these new boulevards that go straight on, without meandering, without the adventures of perspective, implacably straight lines, without any of the atmosphere of Balzac's world, making one think of some American Babylon of the future." He thought it witless to live in a time of growth, when the soul became "as uncomfortable as a body in a damp house." The author Théophile Gautier also felt disheartened: "This is no longer the Paris I used to know. It is Philadelphia, St. Petersburg, anything you like, but not Paris." In the

OPPOSITE: *Exterior detail of the Winn Memorial Public Library, Woburn, Massachusetts, 1876–79. Details such as this convey the sense of reality, weight, and physical presence that Richardson sought in his buildings.*

Main front of the Crane Memorial Library, Quincy, Massachusetts, 1880–82. The Crane is Richardson's most compact library, with "eyebrow" dormers barely interrupting the plane of the roof, a stair tower snuggled within the main gable, and an uninterrupted horizontal ridge against the sky.

view of such unhappy observers, Haussmann exchanged the venerable planning irregularities of medieval Paris for the sterile gridiron of an Americanized future. Although the terms have changed somewhat, it is a cry against American cultural hegemony that echoes down to our day.

All this disruption created a dramatically changed, and changing, urban experience. Although Richardson in Paris lived amid these upheavals, just as he had grown up during the improvements in the Second Municipality in New Orleans, and must have taken some notice of them, he mentions nothing about his surroundings in the few letters that survive from this time. Later, in 1883, when he was vying for the design of a casino and theater in Washington, D.C., he did write to the potential client that he had given "considerable attention and study" while in Paris to the erection of the Opéra. True or not, it seemed a useful thing to say at the time. As a new student of architecture, however, he appears to have kept his eyes on his own goals. Or perhaps he thought it about time Paris came to look like an American Babylon.

When he arrived in the city Richardson needed to find an architectural atelier, or private drafting studio, where he could place himself under the aegis of a *patron*. He had his pick of about a dozen ateliers, including that of Hector Lefuel, which had been the choice of the few previous Americans to attend the École. But Richardson chose the small and relatively new studio of forty-year-old Louis-

Jules André. Jules André had won the coveted *Prix de Rome* in 1847, spent three years studying in Italy at government expense, and began to teach in 1856. His atelier would grow to be much sought after, especially by the increasing number of Americans who followed in Richardson's footsteps.

Once ensconced as a member of the Atelier André, Richardson could apply for admission to the school itself. The École des Beaux-Arts, including the sections devoted to painting and sculpture, on the one hand, and architecture, on the other, occupied the Left Bank site of the former Monastery of the Petits-Augustins on the rue Bonaparte, a location that had also housed a museum of architectural antiquities. By Richardson's time the school existed in buildings adapted, recently erected, or under construction from designs by the architect Félix Duban, who incorporated as accents in the entrance courts fragments of the facades of the Renaissance châteaux of Anet and Gaillon. French classical precedent was everywhere evident. Beyond the forecourts off the rue Bonaparte stood the Palais des Études, whose austerely classical, Renaissance Revival facade masked the library, a collection of casts of antique sculpture, and a hemicycle with Paul Delaroche's dominating representation of the great painters, sculptors, and architects of the past. The government ran the École, a school free of charge and open to any male between fifteen and thirty years of age who could pass its exacting entrance examination.

By November 1859, as an *aspirant* of the school, Richardson had presented his letter of introduction from Jules André and brashly taken—and failed—that exam. Both written and oral, and in French, it plumbed his knowledge of such subjects as mathematics and descriptive geometry. The latter was fundamental to the teaching method of the École. The orals in algebra and plane geometry he narrowly passed, but he had just taken up the arcane study of descriptive geometry, and it defeated him. At registration for the exam Richardson bumped into an Englishman named R. Phené Spiers, who came from a different atelier, run by Charles-Auguste Questel, and who passed the exam. Although Spiers left Paris in 1861, the two architects were to remain lifelong, if long-range, friends.

Richardson had to wait a year to try again for entrance, but as an *aspirant* he could begin to draw in the atelier, use the library on the top floor of the Palais des Études, sketch the casts of sculpture in the Salles des Études Antiques, and listen to lectures. He used these privileges during 1859–60, developing his graphic skills by, among other labors, copying an engraving of a vaulted classical interior from Giambattista Piranesi's *Prima parte di architettura*, which he found in the library, and sketching one of the male nudes from the first-century Roman Ildefonso Group that caught his eye among the casts. Neither of these early drawings shows great achievement in draftsmanship. In fact, Richardson never ranked among the most skilled of graphic artists. As a mature architect his creative focus existed beyond drawing, in the finished building itself.

He took the entrance exam again the next November, in 1860. It lasted the better part of the month, took place in public, and again transpired entirely in French. Illness at one point forced him to submit an unfinished design, and confusion caused by language reduced his score in mathematics, but he otherwise did well. Of the 120 examinees, sixty were admitted, and he finished eighteenth. He became a member of the second class of the École on November 20, 1860.

Once admitted as a student, Richardson may have continued to attend lectures on history, theory, structures, and other subjects. They were optional and, except for those on structure, were largely unattended. The student could proceed at his own speed, but he needed to accumulate credits in both structure and design. To earn promotion from the second to the first class he had to pass four courses in construction, one each in wood, stone, and iron and a general one. Wood and stone were traditional materials used in traditional ways; iron had been introduced as a new structural material in the aftermath of the Industrial Revolution, and it required new calculations. Much nineteenth-century architecture forthrightly expressed the innovative structural materials and the engineering that held them up, but Richardson never embraced this industrial aesthetic.

Architectural composition commanded the most attention at the École. Design problems appeared monthly from the professor of architectural theory. These *concours* were of two kinds: the *esquisse*, a sketch finished in twelve hours, and the *projet rendu*, requiring the development of the *esquisse* into a building design presented in three finished drawings after two months. The latter began with a sketch *en loge*, a twelve-hour closeted period of preliminary development from which a scheme emerged. If the study satisfied the student, he could ripen it, without departing too much from his sketch, under the guidance and criticism of his *patron* and the older members of his atelier. To advance to the first class he needed to receive credit for one or two of these finished projects in a year.

The ateliers grouped in quarters around the École provided the actual design instruction. An experienced architect—often, like Jules André, a Prix de Rome winner—headed the studio, stopping by for formal criticism two or three times a week. The rest of the time other students in various stages of development offered support, the older students instructing the younger, the younger students laboring on the projects of the older. It was teamwork, this collaborative effort under the direction of one designer, and when a project met with success, the entire atelier celebrated. Such teamwork—controlled by the master, of course —remained central to Richardson's later practice.

Richardson's student life revolved around the self-governed atelier. A chosen leader collected the money for rent, heat, and the *patron*'s fee. A new member underwent a rite of initiation, then stood the atelier to food and drink. Richardson had been well trained for such shenanigans at Harvard and probably sailed through this with flying colors.

Exterior of the book room, Winn Memorial Library, Woburn, Massachusetts, 1876–79. Richardson resolved whole or parts of exteriors into a layering of ashlar base, window strip, and sheltering roof to create a repetition of horizontals that was to influence the prairie houses of Frank Lloyd Wright.

At the time he entered, Richardson, as an American, was a rarity among the students, but he was not the first to attend the architectural section of the École des Beaux-Arts. Richard Morris Hunt, most notably, preceded Richardson by a decade, worked for another *patron*, Hector Lefuel, on the new Louvre in the 1850s, then set up practice in New York. Hunt soon became one of the leading architects in the United States, an accomplished practitioner of the French mode, an "ambassador of art from the old world to the new," and a professional colleague and rival of Richardson. Both men eventually established offices on the model of the atelier system they had experienced in Paris. Both men were followed by a legion of American students to the end of the century and beyond. They created mature works, however, that were poles apart stylistically.

Nor was Richardson the only native of Louisiana studying architecture in Paris during 1860–61. James Freret also stemmed from an old New Orleans family. An exact contemporary of Richardson, he had, as was customary in the period, apprenticed to architects in his native city in the late 1850s and practiced briefly on his own before traveling to Europe in June 1860. According to a later promotional notice, he spent thirteen months at the École and the Atelier Questel (where, we remember, Richardson's friend Phené Spiers worked), then traveled through Switzerland, France, and England. No official record reports that Freret ever gained entrance to the École itself, but as we have seen, it was possible to draft in an atelier without that formality. His later drawings certainly suggest a period of French training. Nor do we know whether he and Richardson met each other—although it is hardly conceivable that they did not—but, as we shall see, Freret's biography forms an instructive contrast to Richardson's own history during this period.

Unlike Freret, when Richardson arrived in Paris he had had no previous experience in design. Even by the time he entered the École, late in 1860, he was not ready to produce acceptable architectural drawings—indeed, it took him two years to receive his first credit for a project. In his first seven months he entered every *concours* but dropped out of five and received no credit for the other two. New students of design often meet with little success, but in Richardson's case his early record probably reflected preoccupation with events at home more than a lack of design experience—for after months of saber rattling, the Civil War began with the bombardment of Fort Sumter on April 12, 1861. There followed a long gap in Richardson's academic record.

During that gap Richardson struggled mightily with his conscience. For his compatriot James Freret, who had never lived in the North, the war suggested just one course of action. He returned to the South, ran the blockade of Charleston in August 1862, fought for the Confederacy, and was disabled at the Battle of Port Arthur. After the war he returned to a productive career in his native city. In contrast, the war set in painful conflict Richardson's feelings for his natal and his adopted homes. Mounting stress required some sort of release, and that came in the form of a pointless and frustrating round trip across the Atlantic. After stewing over the summer, in late September 1861 he left Paris not for Charleston or New Orleans but for Boston, via England. By early October he was in London, staying with Henry Adams at the American legation, where Adams served as secretary to his father, the minister to the Court of St. James. On the fifth Richardson sailed from Liverpool on board the Cunarder *Arabia*, a wooden, two-masted paddle steamer, and he landed in Boston on the seventeenth.

There he found himself an alien, an enemy alien, without a valid passport. He occupied "a horrible position," according to Adams. "His family and property are in New Orleans. He is himself a good Union man, I believe . . . but he does not want to do anything which will separate him from his family or make them his enemies." His dilemma took on professional as well as personal dimensions. He tried to find architectural work in Boston, but, it was said, he could not accept the conditions offered. It should also be recognized that he was scarcely trained for the job. Richardson thought of going to Louisiana, but friends counseled that it would ruin his career. He held an untenable position, especially as he had refused to take an oath to the Union out of consideration for his family. After a winter of discontent, he returned to France.

In exile he was intellectually reconciled to a neutral position but emotionally still very fragile. He reached Paris in mid-March with "mingled feelings of

Book alcoves, Winn Memorial Library, Woburn, Massachusetts, 1876–79. Richardson's library designs placed books at arm's reach, rather than storing them away in closed stacks as was becoming standard practice by the 1870s.

OPPOSITE: *Exterior, Winn Memorial Library, Woburn, Massachusetts, 1876–79. This, Richardson's earliest library, so captivated Frederick Billings that he asked the architect to design the library he donated to the University of Vermont.*

Reading–room detail, Winn Memorial Library, Woburn, Massachusetts, 1876–79. The weary reader can rest eyes on such exquisitely designed details as this foliate capital in one of the alcoves.

joy and sorrow," he told Julia. "Politics I wash my hands of, externally at least," he wrote his fiancée at the end of the month. He buried his conflict as he was later to deny his chronic illness. "He never . . . appeared to have politics very much on his mind," remembered Josiah Bradlee, one of his former classmates, then studying music in Paris. "At any rate there was no bitter partisan feeling—indeed, bitterness was not in the man." He continued to balance opposing feelings; or, as Henry Adams noted as late as the fall of the next year, politically he still sat "on the fence."

The cost of his outward composure must have been an inward struggle the extent of which we can only guess. His younger brother, William Priestley Richardson, who also had friends both North and South but no promising career to protect, left Harvard to join the Confederate army in 1862. He rose to the rank of captain in the 13th Louisiana Infantry, survived some of the fiercest battles of the war, at Shiloh, Chattanooga, and Vicksburg, and spent the last days of the conflict as a prisoner of the North. In a letter written to H. H. after the hostilities, he expressed no bitterness toward his brother, but he continued to champion the rightness of the Southern struggle. "The most just cause sword was ever drawn for, has failed," he wrote, "and we have become unwilling subjects of the worse despotism the world ever saw."

The architectural student probably had little news of his brother during the conflict, but even in Paris he knew the fate of New Orleans and, by extension, his family. On April 17, 1862, Richardson wrote to Julia: "Operations have been commenced against New Orleans. I feel nervous and anxious to hear more. Poor mother and sisters—if I thought I could in any way aid them . . . I would go tomorrow." By mid-May he knew the city had fallen to David Farragut's armada and now lay "governed by strangers," under the thumb of inept Gen. Benjamin F. Butler of Massachusetts. To the South, "Beast" Butler's occupation of the city amounted to a reign of terror. "What a position to be placed in," Richardson lamented to Julia. "How I have suffered and do suffer" because of divided loyalties, "no one can ever know." He would endure the greatest sacrifices for his friends in Boston, but he also "burned with shame when I read the capture of my city and I in Paris." But even his mother wrote to tell him to stay where he was.

The fall of New Orleans affected him not only emotionally but financially. Despite his stepfather's protestation of poverty, Richardson had up to this point lived "with ease," free of care about financial matters. His status changed noticeably, then dramatically in the spring of 1862, but this was foreseeable much sooner. As early as mid-August 1861, four months after the firing on Fort Sumter, Richardson's former classmate and traveling companion Frederic d'Hautville wrote to say that it had suddenly occurred to him that Richardson may have been unable to receive regular remittances from home. He had $500 he could spare and would be *"enchanted"* to lend it. "I give you 25 years to pay it in, or if that wont [*sic*] do take 50 years." D'Hautville was one of those Boston friends for whom Richardson would willingly have undergone great sacrifices. "For their kindness I owe an everlasting debt," he had written to Julia. We can see why.

We do not know whether Richardson accepted d'Hautville's offer, but after his return to Paris in 1862 he wondered if his family's agent in Liverpool held money he could draw on. If not, he said, he would immediately begin to support himself. Apparently no funds existed in England. A week later he wrote Julia to say that he had given up all hope of aid from home and would begin the next week to work for his living.

Reduced circumstances also show up in his changing addresses. He had left the pension in the rue de Vaugirard the previous year and taken a pleasant apartment in the rue de Luxembourg, between the Place Vendôme and the Madeleine on the other side of the Seine. He might then reach the École and his atelier by an exhilarating walk across the Place de la Concorde, the Pont de la Concorde, and along the Quai d'Orsay, meanwhile passing some of the city's greatest classical architecture. He now moved again, to less expensive quarters back on the Left Bank, to a room "in the not very attractive rue Mazarin," according to Joe Bradlee. Later he roomed in an attic on the rue du Bac, leading to the Pont Royal, with a French atelier mate, Gustave-Adolphe Gerhardt. In these various moves he circled his centers of interest, the École and the Atelier André.

Before his funds were cut off, Richardson continued to display the love of fine dress that characterized him at Harvard. A series of *carte de visite* photographs taken in Montmarte in March 1861 show him nattily attired in dark frock coat and stovepipe hat, sporting a walking stick, and surrounded by artistic studio props. He presented himself as the very image of an art student during the Second Empire. Even during his bolt for Boston that autumn, both coming and going he found the time, energy, and money to stop at Poole's, then as now the fashionable Savile Row tailors in London, to refurbish his wardrobe. On October 4 he spent nearly nineteen pounds for "a blue milled melton lounging coat" with silk-lined

Reading room, Winn Memorial Library, Woburn, Massachusetts, 1876–79. Although public institutions, Richardson's libraries drew inspiration from private gentlemen's libraries, with custom-designed chairs drawn up for reading before a warming fireplace.

sleeves, "a fancy buck skin lounging vest," and buckskin trousers. On his return in March of the next year he again shopped for clothes, buying a silk-lined "blue Berlin frock coat" and "black melton trousers" for nine and a half pounds. As long as his funds held out, he continued to live in the spirit of his undergraduate nickname, the tongue-in-cheek "Nothing to Wear."

Richardson in his early twenties seemed "a slender youth of promising talent, a good-tempered and amiable companion," according to Joe Bradlee's reminiscences. The *carte-de-visite* photographs show him as indeed lean. His expression is serious, his eyes intense, and his wedge-shaped head supports a luxuriant growth of dark wavy hair. He is a very handsome lad. As at Cambridge, he continued to enjoy easy friendships, now with both Frenchmen and a few Americans. Paris held some American pals like Bradlee. Henry Adams occasionally came over from London to seek out Richardson on the rue du Bac or elsewhere and take him to dine at the Palais Royal, where they talked about whatever interested art students. Not that Adams understood what he was told, for he insisted that everything French was bad except the restaurants. For a while he chummed with Phené Spiers. French atelier mates Adolphe Gerhardt and Julien Guadet became his friends. (There remains to this day in the Avery Library at Columbia University an album of photographs of École projects inscribed to Richardson, probably in 1864, by Guadet, Gerhardt, and another colleague named Ambroise Baudry.) Many of these men became important architects or educators, and all stayed in touch with him.

H. H. Richardson in Paris, 1861. One of a series of carte-de-visite *photographs taken during Richardson's early days as a student at the École des Beaux-Arts.*

Proving his stepfather's faith in him well placed, Richardson in Paris added a seriousness of purpose to the fun-loving character who had entered Harvard, although it should be recognized that most of what we know of his life there comes from the comments of friends written after his death. Later success proves that he did indeed apply himself, but it is difficult to imagine him eschewing all of Paris's pleasures. Bradlee reported that Richardson never allowed dinner or dancing parties to interfere with his work, that he frequently left these gatherings early so he could finish the night in study or drafting. This became especially true after his return from Boston in March 1862. "Paris is to a man what college is to a boy," he wrote Julia. "I think Paris a dangerous place to send a young man." But he was writing to his fiancée and he needed to reassure her. In another letter he said that the city had "no charms for me except my studies." And he added in another, "Study and society are incompatible." It does seem to be a fact that after Richardson came back to Paris from Boston he assumed a very busy schedule, eventually drafting by day in architec-

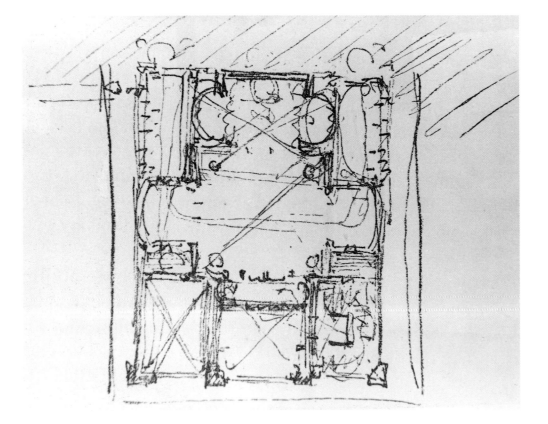

tural offices to earn his keep and working on his own École *concours* as well as projects for his mates in the atelier by night to improve his skills. If Gerhardt is to be believed, he even found time to study painting with Alfred Leperre. "No one can say that I waste my time," he wrote.

Between the end of 1862 and the end of 1864, the jury at the École accepted nine problems from Richardson, three in architecture, one in mathematics, four in construction, and one in perspective. He never achieved a mark higher than passing (there was no grade inflation at the École), but he nonetheless ranked "good" in comparison to most of his fellow students. He had worked on other projects that he left unfinished or that went unrewarded, such as the design for a "Corps Legislatif," or legislative assembly hall, about which he wrote to Julia in April 1862. The judges rejected his graphic solution to that problem in June. Thirty-eight times in forty-one months he picked up a design program, sketching private and public buildings, civic and commercial structures. Since he remained a student in the lower class, these were all relatively simple tasks.

On June 3, 1863, Richardson drew an *esquisse* for a casino on the promenade of a resort where visitors came to drink the water for medicinal purposes. The project included areas for recreation and study. His thumbnail plan, which he did not submit for judgment, configured the various elements of the program into a simple diagram: a cross within a rectangular outer perimeter. This is a characteristic École arrangement of primary and secondary spaces axially and hierarchically ordered. In his rapid analysis and synthesis of the elements of the building program, Richardson created a controlled and highly legible architectural composition, a method of design he developed and followed for the rest of his life.

Richardson did not labor only on his own *concours*. In the atelier a student helped in the presentation of projects by others, especially in the annual competitions for the Prix de Rome. The École awarded no diplomas. Either a student moved directly on to professional work or the coveted Rome Prize marked the culmination of a winner's education—if he was French, for as a government stipend it was not open to foreigners. During Richardson's tenure in the Atelier André, two of his colleagues won the prize: Julien Guadet in 1864 and Adolphe Gerhardt in 1865. Certainly he knew and perhaps helped to present these winning projects. As roommate as well as atelier mate, Richardson must have worked on the drawings for Gerhardt's design for a hotel on a Swiss lake, but Guadet's project seems to have had greater impact upon him. Guadet, more gifted as theoretician than as designer despite his Rome Prize, later taught at the École and published the definitive work on its method of design. Classicism reigned in the ateliers, but instruction emphasized both a rational organization of the building program and a sequential planning process, using rooms arranged in order of importance and balanced along axes.

André in particular impressed upon his pupils "bigness," "broad contrasts of light and shadow," and "largeness of detail." The parti, or schema, of Guadet's winning design for a hospice in the Alps was characteristic of École projects. It shows an astylar (columnless) Romanesque mountaintop monastery whose horizontal layers pyramid upward toward a central church with axial tower and spire. Round-arched arcades articulate the broad exterior walls of the building blocks. The section through the church displays an interior almost Byzantine in its richly polychromatic, geometrical, and figural decorative scheme. This project must have deeply impressed Richardson, for he varied its parti and its details over and over again in his mature buildings.

During these years the young American architect, we are told, worked a grueling schedule, which at least at one point affected his health. He labored long hours at his and others' projects, determined to absorb as much as he could. The more he learned, the more committed to the profession he became, the "nobler" it seemed, the "more majesty" it gained. If there were moments when Richardson's determination waned, he might have visited Delaroche's painting in the Salle des Prix and drawn strength from the representations of his great predecessors. He had no interest in becoming a second-class architect, and he intended to study hard to insure his success. "If I persevere I must succeed in the end, and my profession will be much dearer to me from the very pain it has caused me," he told Julia, projecting a youthful idealism. He professed to be unconcerned about his lack of money and regretted any time he was not at his studies.

Richardson studied at the École in a time of change. One historian described the 1860s as a "tumultuous and fruitful decade" at the school. Indeed, as in the sixties a century later, there must have been periods in which little work was

possible because of student unrest. The nineteenth-century battle of the styles, of the Classicists versus the Romanticists, spilled over into the precinct of the École and the ateliers. A clash between academic Classicists and emerging and powerfully backed Gothicists led to an Act of Reorganization, decreed by Napoleon III in November 1863, that tried, and ultimately failed, to reform the school's teaching. Eugène-Emmanuel Viollet-le-Duc, architect, archeologist, theoretician, author, neo-Goth, and instigator of the reform movement, joined the faculty the next year. As another historian has put it, "the foremost medievalist was to be enthroned in the most classical of schools." He seemed, predictably, a square peg in a round hole and a "trampler on traditions," according to the obituary of Peter B. Wight. During each of the dull but required lectures he delivered between January and March 1864, the students hissed, hooted, and stomped; after each of them, they rioted in the streets surrounding the École. Viollet-le-Duc wisely resigned after the aborted series.

Despite his busy schedule, Richardson apparently took part in—or was in the vicinity of—at least one public demonstration against the proposed new order and as a result landed in an overnight lockup, notwithstanding his status

Interior of Trinity Church, Copley Square, Boston, 1872–77. The splendid interior of Trinity is a descendant of a prize-winning project for a church at a hospice in the Alps that Richardson helped work on for his colleague Julien Guadet when Richardson was a student at the École des Beaux-Arts in Paris.

as a foreigner. One version of the story says that a group of students signed a statement of protest in Richardson's room, after which he accompanied them to deliver it to the emperor at the Tuileries and was arrested while watching the demonstration. According to another version, however, Richardson was a prime mover in the uprising and joined the crowd that "drove the lecturer across the Pont des Arts."

In any event he was thrown into jail, where his personal appearance—produced as he himself explained by those "good clothes from Poole's" he had bought in London—earned him the right to share a cell with a "strange-looking, long-haired gentleman of enchanting conversational powers." This proved to be the distinguished author and poet Théophile Gautier. As a member of the Committee of Instruction of the École, Gautier attended Viollet's first lecture, a lecture at which the students created an uproar, but apparently no one has explained why the poet landed in jail. Richardson's story has it that the minister of fine arts himself, the comte de Nieuwerkerke, set both Richardson and Gautier free the next morning, with the foreign student proudly walking out between the decorated official and the famous poet. Our knowledge of this encounter stems only from the architect himself, who told it to Mariana Van Rensselaer and others "in those rapid words which were emphasized into greater piquancy by his slightly stammering tongue."

In his later telling of this event Richardson insisted that he protested

Main front of the Converse Memorial Library, Malden, Massachusetts, 1883–85. After his return from Paris, Richardson adapted historical European architectural forms to create conservative, personal, and highly influential buildings.

OPPOSITE: *Detail of the exterior arcade of the Converse Memorial Library, Malden, Massachusetts, 1883–85. Droll ornamental details of a kind common in the Romanesque architecture of France and Spain often enliven Richardson's buildings.*

against the government interference in the affairs of the school, not the lecturer himself, but he never championed Viollet-le-Duc's design theories, nor did he embrace either the Gothic style or the industrial aesthetic advanced by the Frenchman. In his theoretical writings Viollet advocated an architecture based upon both the past and the present, upon both history and industrialization. This architecture, he demonstrated, would be one that utilized his own interpretation of Gothic structure as rational in system and thrifty in its use of materials, but replaced the stonework of the cathedrals with the ironwork of the modern industrial age. Viollet-le-Duc's ideas had an important influence on late-nineteenth-century architecture in Europe and the United States. As Richardson's mature work demonstrates, however, he wanted nothing to do with either Gothic or iron architecture.

Nonetheless, several of the Frenchman's books sat in his library. He bought them and others with money he could not spare. In Paris Richardson laid the foundation of what was to become a professional collection of books. This included, among others, Viollet's multivolume *Dictionnaire* and his *Entretiens*, or lectures; Léon Château's history of French architecture; a work on building technology; Paul Letarouilly's *Édifices de Rome Moderne;* Victor Petit on the châteaux of the Loire; and Verdier and Cattois's *Architecture civile et domestique au moyen âge et à la renaissance.* Richardson probably bought English architectural books on his passages through London. He owned several titles written or inspired by John Ruskin, and he certainly read Ruskin's *Seven Lamps of Architecture* and his *Stones of Venice* in early editions. There was nothing special about such a library of French and English books. Richardson collected the standard reference works for his upcoming professional practice, and he drew upon this resource—to which he continued to add—throughout his career.

Richardson, as a student and later, read not only professional publications but histories and popular literature. At Harvard, as we have seen, he bought popular English novels of the day. Later in life, according to Van Rensselaer, he liked to relax with the works of the French author Émile Gaboriau, the so-called father of the detective novel. Gaboriau's publications, such as *L'Affaire Lerouge* of 1865, began to appear in Paris during Richardson's student days, so it is probably safe to say that he discovered the author then and pursued his habit of reading for relaxation even during the busy months of his exile.

Once Richardson realized that he was cut off from funds from home, he also realized he would have to work to support himself, and the trip to Boston had proven that he would have to remain in Paris to find work. By mid-July 1862 he had done just that. With the help of his *patron,* Jules André, he joined the office of Théodore Labrouste, another Prix de Rome winner and one of the principal government architects of the time. Richardson worked on the drawings for Labrouste's Hospice des Incurables at Ivry, a complex containing two thousand beds, a large church, and a nunnery. He may also have found employment with Jacques Hittorff, whose iron-built railroad station, the Gare du Nord, was under construction during Richardson's Parisian years. Richardson's later work suggests that he learned more from the planning problems posed by the vast hospital than from the modern structural materials of the railroad station, for he was never to use metallic construction in any significantly visible, architectural way.

Meaningful work for sustaining wages lifted his spirits a great deal. And practical experience in the world of real building, of hospitals and railroad stations, augmented the idealism of paper-bound École projects for mineral spas and mountaintop monasteries. Richardson's stay in Paris made of him, as it had of his predecessor Richard Morris Hunt, an architect thoroughly grounded in the theory and practice of his profession.

Like Hunt and other men to follow, Richardson might have returned to the United States to build in the prevailing French academic classical style. "It would not cost me a bit of trouble," he later told Mariana Van Rensselaer, "to build French buildings" from Boston to Philadelphia. "But that is not what I want to do." Instead, Richardson developed into a cosmopolitan rather than a Francophile during his student years. Despite his French training he had seen new buildings in England that he admired, and he became at least as partial to the neomedievalism of the British as to the neoclassicism of the French, although his mature work would stand out from the buildings of either school. His stay in Paris developed within him a logical method of design and a deep appreciation for—but not a slavish attitude toward—the history of architecture. During the next two decades he evolved a distinctly American and a distinctly personal and influential architecture.

5 ❖ NEW YORK 1865–74

THE END OF THE AMERICAN CIVIL WAR MEANT THE END OF RICHARD-son's Parisian exile. He returned to the United States just after his twenty-seventh birthday, in October 1865. Years earlier he had written to his fiancée that with the proper training he could set up practice anywhere. When the time came, his options were indeed varied. He could choose from such places as Paris, where colleagues urged him to become a French citizen and try for a Prix de Rome; New Orleans, from which his family wrote to predict renewed prosperity in need of architectural services; Boston, where friends promised a lively social milieu; New York, where he might find a fresh start; and even Mexico City, where Emperor Maximilian seemed (falsely, as events were all too quickly to prove) steady on a throne supported by the emperor of France. Richardson's decision in favor of New York rather than New Orleans or Boston probably reflected his continuing ambivalence about his loyalties during the war. New York must have seemed a neutral corner, one that also appeared to offer his best career options.

Again we glimpse his struggle, but can only guess at its intensity. Although Van Rensselaer reports that he had a constant wish to return to New Orleans, after college he never again visited his native city. There was, however, no break with his family there. Members North and South exchanged letters, and the Southerners came North for visits or business. Once he had opted for the North, however, Richardson never looked back. He soon numbered among his clients and friends veterans of the Union army, many of whom had been his old Harvard buddies, and he even found it possible to design Union war memorials for Worcester, Massachusetts, Buffalo, and Boston. Phillips Brooks emphasized Richardson's Southern upbringing, observing that "nobody can understand him or his career who does not keep that fact always in mind," but he also wrote bluntly that "the war was over, and there was work to do."

In New York Richardson laid the foundations for both his family life and his architectural practice. In the nine years between the end of the Civil War and the depression of the early 1870s, he married, sired five of his six children, met many of his principal collaborators, and developed professionally from a highly trained but obscure draftsman into the envied designer of Trinity Church in Boston, one of the most important architectural commissions in the country. He also began to form his own architectural style. The city may have been a mere halfway point in

OPPOSITE: *Exterior of the chancel and tower, Grace Church, Medford, Massachusetts. Richardson's early works exhibit the expected revival styles of the day such as the English Gothic.*

his journey back to New England, but it proved to be a most important stopover along the way.

The city of New York in 1865 barely existed above Forty-second Street in Manhattan, despite the fact that the new park stretching northward from Fifty-ninth Street was called "Central." Overcrowding characterized the city below Forty-second Street. An observer in 1866 likened Manhattan to a boy who had outgrown his clothes, bursting as it was at the seams. "The scarcity of houses, and the costs of rent, living, and taxation, are . . . driving a large portion of our middling class into the country," he wrote. And we think of the middle-class flight from the city as a phenomenon of our own day.

During Richardson's tenure the city grew outward, and the development of transportation by widening, straightening, or building streets, by engineering bridges, by constructing railroads and elevateds, or by floating ferries became a prime concern. The Roeblings' great bridge joining Manhattan to Brooklyn, begun in 1869 and slowly taking shape during Richardson's New York days, symbolized this centrifugal energy as well as the progressive direction of the new industrial technology. And the city grew upward with the application of new mechanical services such as the safe passenger elevator and the introduction of "French flats," or tall apartment blocks, designed by Richard Morris Hunt and others.

Richardson should have been used to all this urban uproar from his boyhood in the developing American Sector of New Orleans or his stay in Haussmann's Paris, but he may have had his fill of it by then, for he left no mention of any of these urban improvements. Nor did he settle in Manhattan to witness the boom; he joined the flight to the suburbs—to Connecticut, New Jersey, Long Island, or, in his case, to Staten Island.

Richardson shunned the center, shunned the corruption of Boss Tweed and his gang, shunned the battles between the Catholic Irish and the Orangemen that erupted from time to time, and it cannot be demonstrated that he took any interest in the conquest of nature by the Brooklyn Bridge or other great feats of urban-industrial transformation of the day. He joined the upswelling migration out of the commercial core and, eventually, into the leafy suburbs. And when he left suburban New York, he moved to suburban Boston.

On his return to the States he first took a room in a boardinghouse across the East River in Brooklyn. One of his fellow boarders was a woman who remembered him vividly. Then "of good height, broad-shouldered, full-chested, dark complexion, brown eyes, dark hair parted in the centre," she reported, he "had the look of a man in perfect health and with much physical vigor." He dressed in the morning and thought no more of his appearance: in well-tailored clothes worn with "an indescribable air of ease," carelessly tied cravats, "thick, broad-soled" brogans that looked more English than French. He preferred to speak French rather than English, but spoke them both with a stammer. He rolled and smoked his own cigarettes, liked hash for breakfast, and coffee "so strong that you can never wash the cup white after using."

After a few months of boardinghouse life, in the spring of 1866 our unnamed informant decided to move with her son to a house on Staten Island, and Richardson went with them. He took over a small back parlor, unpacked his library, and continued to study and draw. There he regaled his landlady and her son with tales of life in Paris, some a mite fanciful perhaps, and praised the generosity of the friends who had helped him there. Daily cold-water baths and long walks kept him fit. He grieved at the death of his mother in distant Louisiana, but, significantly, went for consolation to Julia in Boston rather than to his family in New Orleans.

Richardson's first year back left a rather bleak record. Money was scarce; starts proved false. At one point he even tried to get work at Tiffany's "shaping and ornamenting gas-shades." He joined forces with a builder named Roberts whom he had met in Paris, but the association ended early. Although the men had not seen eye to eye, they nonetheless parted friends. Richardson thought it a good thing, really, and prepared for a period of struggle, but his innate optimism gave him confidence in his eventual success. For a while he formed another partnership, with the architect E. J. Little, but that too ended quickly. He told his landlady he was broke. "Something favorable will turn up," she said. "Stay on with us."

Richardson was not one to give in to the sorrows attendant on low funds and forced idleness. Nor did he hide alone in his room. His cousin the paper manufacturer and erstwhile editor John Priestley sponsored his membership in the Century Association, a fashionable social center for writers, artists, and amateurs of letters and the other arts, where one gained admission through "brains, culture, and achievement"—or, in Richardson's case, distinguished ancestry and potential achievement. The Century put the aspiring architect in touch with the city's elite.

Departing for the Century Association clubhouse on East Fifteenth Street in Manhattan one evening, Richardson confided to his landlady that he wore a suit tailored by Poole's and fit for a nobleman, "and—and—and," he stuttered, "I haven't a dollar to my name." Like his famous successor Frank Lloyd Wright, the architect early on displayed a knack for spending money he did not have. Indeed, Richardson's shopping at Poole's in London on his way back home from Paris had added nearly thirty-seven pounds' worth of apparel to his wardrobe.

When Richardson split with Roberts he knew he was in for a struggle and hoped he would soon find work. "All I want now is an order," he wrote. That order appeared near the end of the year, in November 1866, and it came through the influence of his old Harvard mate and traveling companion James A. Rumrill. Rumrill's father, also James, and his father-in-law, Chester W. Chapin Sr., were the chief backers of a new church for the Unitarian organization in Springfield,

H. H. Richardson, Church of the Unity, Springfield, Massachusetts, 1866–69. The architect's first building, this Gothic Unitarian church was demolished in 1960.

Massachusetts. Sixty-eight-year-old Chapin was a banker, railroad executive, and later United States congressman who did much to develop the transportation systems of the western part of his state. He later commissioned one of Richardson's collaborators, the sculptor Augustus Saint-Gaudens, to model the statue of *The Pilgrim* that now stands near the Public Library in Springfield. The younger Rumrill followed him into the railroad field, and this was not the last commission he would throw his friend's way. Through his urging, the church asked Richardson to compete for the design of its new building, and through his influence, and over the objections of a member of the building committee who worried that Richardson was untried and hence not the man for so important a trust, he won that competition.

Rumrill's support, bolstered perhaps by Richardson's own distinguished Unitarian background, got Richardson his first commission at the age of twenty-eight. With his design for the Church of the Unity he began his career in service to a Unitarian congregation. Great-grandfather Priestley would have been proud.

Despite the architect's French training, the church for Springfield looked primarily English. Country Gothic in style, following the reform ideas of men such as A. W. N. Pugin and John Ruskin, it looked like any number of ecclesiastical structures the architect might have seen on one of his trips through England. The building rose as an asymmetrical composition of narthex with pointed arcade, tower with octagonal broach spire, hammer-beamed nave, and Sunday school room. The exterior of East Longmeadow stone, from just outside the city, laid up in random ashlar, assumed a pattern that would form part of the architect's signature. The building stood animated and colorful.

Richardson believed in "bold, rich, living architecture," as he told his landlady when he showed her the drawings for the Springfield church. And he gave warning to future clients by adding that he did not like it when the architect was "fettered by lack of money in the builder." He showed he knew his Ruskin, especially the chapter called "Lamp of Sacrifice" in his copy of the English critic's *Seven Lamps of Architecture*, when he added that he thought the best use of money was "to spend it in architecture to which posterity may point with pride." Alas, we can now point merely to the empty site where the church once stood, for it was demolished in 1960.

The Springfield church launched Richardson's career. There was no reason now to prolong his engagement to Julia Gorham Hayden, the daughter of Dr. and Mrs. John Cole Hayden of Boston, who was a year older than he. She had waited patiently since early 1859, a period of nearly eight years during which she had seen rather little of him. She was, it seems, a woman of constant hope and great patience. They married in Boston in early January 1867, traveled through Springfield to visit the Rumrills, then settled into a rented cottage on Staten Island during one of the coldest winters on record. In April Julia wrote a long, chatty letter to her mother detailing the quotidian events of her newly married life, a period before the babies started to arrive. She reported much to-ing and fro-ing of visitors, including the Rumrills and the neighboring Redmonds, who wanted Richardson to design them a Staten Island house. She had to train the new maid. And she fretted about "Hal," who was often gone to his office in the city or to Springfield or Boston. She had not written in some time because she was busy during the day and "in the evening Hal is at home & wants my attention"—perhaps to listen to him play the flute, for in another letter she asked her mother to send "Hal's music."

Julia was a narrowly circumscribed homebody typical of the middle-class wives of the era. At just this moment the bilious journalist Ambrose Bierce wrote in the *San Francisco Californian* (a little cruelly perhaps, as was his way) that a woman's "babies and her visitors are about her only society; and . . . neither are particularly well-calculated to give her broad views or mental culture." That remark could have applied to Julia and countless other women of the time. Descendants remembered her as shy, and at the time of her husband's death, his colleague Frederick Law Olmsted described her as "an admirable woman of child-like simplicity, strong, brave, efficient." Olmsted thought of her as the "kindest of friends." Richardson, he surmised, "could not have been happier in a wife"; but, we must add, the gregarious architect sought intellectual stimulation among males and outside the home.

This is perhaps as good a time as any to confront the tradition that Richardson had a mistress, a rumor that has floated down through some male family members. In the current climate such an ornament is almost required in the biography of any successful man, of any artist, but there seems to be no firm evidence to sustain the idea. It is always possible that Richardson had affairs behind Julia's back. But there is no hard evidence. Indeed, every other indicator suggests that the architect was on the whole a loving husband and father, giving his family what attention he could spare from his all-consuming practice. As P. B. Wight wrote in his obituary, he was a "thoroughly domestic man" devoted "wholly, absolutely and solely" to his work.

Not all his energy went into that work, however, for his family began to expand immediately. Julia Hayden Richardson, or Jula, arrived before the end of 1867. (Over the next nine years she would be joined by five siblings.) With the addition of the baby, the rented cottage began to give at the seams, so in 1868 Richardson designed a wood-framed mansarded house for a site at Clifton, near

H. H. Richardson, H. H. Rich-
ardson house, Staten Island, New
York, 1868–69. The architect
designed this French mansarded
house and lived there with his
growing family and a mortgage
from 1869 to 1874.

the end of the present Verrazano Narrows Bridge on Staten Island. It was a rather common design for the time, although the porch, or "piazza," off both the parlor and the dining room, was rather larger than usual and, as we shall see, may reflect ideas about outdoor living shared at this period by Richardson and Olmsted.

Richardson's father-in-law, perhaps reluctantly, lent the couple part of the cost of building the house. Dr. John Hayden thought it handsome and convenient and agreed with the architect that his professional prospects were good, but he also said that Richardson's decision to build it "was premature and a mistake de-cidedly—it cost too much—it worries him very much." Still, Dr. Hayden thought, with Richardson's income and great prudence he could "meet the expenses of his family and the interest on the cost," if his creditors would give him time.

The Richardsons moved to Massachusetts from their Staten Island house in the spring of 1874, but when the architect died intestate a dozen years later, he left unpaid a second mortgage on the place, still in the hands of Dr. Hayden's heirs (who, of course, numbered his wife among them). They sold the house at public auction a year after his death.

Julia gave birth to four more children during the family's residence in the

Staten Island mansard. John Cole Hayden, named for his maternal grandfather and called "Hayd," joined his sister Jula in 1869. Then came Mary Houghton in 1871, Henry Hyslop in 1872, and Philip in 1874. The sixth child, Frederick Leopold William, arrived in Brookline in 1876. His name derived from those of his father's collaborators and a client at the Capitol in Albany: Frederick Law Olmsted, Leopold Eidlitz, and William Dorsheimer. Jula eventually married the architect George Shepley, and Philip and Frederick both practiced the profession. So began a line of family architects that lasts to the present day.

Richardson's association with Frederick Law Olmsted began on Staten Island in 1866; actually, it may have begun even earlier, for they were both living in Brooklyn boardinghouses until they moved across the Hudson at almost the same moment in late April. Forty-four-year-old Olmsted had lived a diverse and eventful, if somewhat unresolved, career. Seafarer to China at age twenty-one, a gentleman farmer in Connecticut and on Staten Island during his late twenties and early thirties, author of a series of unsurpassed books on the antebellum South that culminated in *The Cotton Kingdom* of 1861, he had in partnership with Calvert Vaux won the competition for the design of Central Park in 1858. During the war he served as general secretary to the United States Sanitary Commission, charged with overseeing medical services and supply distribution to the Union army. Then followed a sojourn to California, where he managed the Mariposa gold mine and drafted a position paper on Yosemite that anticipated the national park movement. About the time he became friends with Richardson, Olmsted had returned to New York to supervise his project for Central Park and to design Prospect Park in Brooklyn. From then on he would concentrate on this field, becoming in the following years the most important landscape architect in the country (and perhaps in his country's history).

Olmsted had been among the most vocal critics of the Old South and Richardson reportedly remained unapologetic about his slaveholding family, but the men grew to be the best of friends. Indeed, they became sufficiently close for Olmsted eventually to follow Richardson when he later moved to Brookline, Massachusetts. While they were personal friends they also associated professionally, collaborating on any number of commissions over the architect's lifetime. And Olmsted—sixteen years Richardson's senior—acted as something of a mentor to the architect in the field of environmental design.

Olmsted was an intellectual, one of the most important in nineteenth-century America, a man who logically and verbally justified his every design decision and who left voluminous writings. Richardson, on the other hand, worked in materials, not words. He was "instinctive and spontaneous . . . not a man of theories" according to Phillips Brooks. "His life passed into his buildings by ways too subtle even for himself to understand." Those buildings eventually reflected the larger social and environmental issues that preoccupied Olmsted. According to his biographer Mariana Van Rensselaer, the architect turned to Olmsted for advice "even in those cases where it seemed as though it could have little practical bearing upon his design."

In May 1870 the New York State Legislature appointed a Staten Island Improvement Commission, charged with initiating proposals for developing the area into an ideal domestic retreat from the city. At the time it was an island in decline, an area noted primarily for its unhealthy environment. Malaria—whose propagation by mosquito was not yet understood—scared away many settlers, although not Olmsted and not Richardson, whose New Orleans upbringing must have hardened him to the dangers of pestilence. After an abortive beginning by others, Olmsted formed a committee of experts to advise the Improvement Commission. In this he included Dr. Elisha Harris, sanitary superintendent of the New York Metropolitan District, Joseph M. Trowbridge, a civil engineer, and H. H. Richardson. In a letter written late in September, Olmsted called the architect "a gentleman trained in the most thorough French technical school, familiar with European road and sanitary engineering, and of highly cultivated taste with a strongly practical direction." Richardson, persuasive as always, must have convinced Olmsted that he had indeed paid attention to Haussmann's rebuilding.

The committee report was written by Olmsted, published in January of the next year, and largely ignored. It projected an ideal suburban community that, in some of its details, seems to suggest the direction of Richardson's early ideas about domestic architecture. Noting the area's reputation for malaria and its faulty ferry service to Manhattan as among its problems, the report advanced a fourteen-point program for improvement in transportation, drainage, public health, housing, water supply, and open space. Houses should be spaced far enough apart so that the air around each "shall be absolutely free from contamination." The inhabitants could then spend a great deal of time outside in order to preserve good health and high morals. This last remark sounds like Olmsted, although out-of-door living was probably more familiar to the Southern-born architect than the New England–born landscapist, but what follows seems certainly to have Louisiana roots. Every house, according to the report, should have a "series of out-of-door apartments, not open to public view, in which direct exposure to sun and wind may, when desired, be avoided." These areas were to be used for ordinary household occupations, so there should be, among other provisions, a "sheltered sitting place for conversation, needle work, reading, teaching, and meditation." Here we see reincarnated the antebellum St. James Parish courtyard, the place of outdoor domestic gathering for Valcour Aime and his family, reworked for the Northern suburbs.

Richardson lived on Staten Island, but he worked on Manhattan, crossing Upper New York Bay morning and evening by that unreliable ferryboat. (Early commuting was an inexact science.) In October 1867 he formed a limited partner-

Exterior of Grace Church, Medford, Massachusetts, 1867–69. This, Richardson's oldest standing building, survives from the beginning of his practice in New England.

ship with Charles Dexter Gambrill, with offices in the Wall Street area, first at 6 Hanover Street and then at 57 Broadway. Boston-born Gambrill had graduated from Harvard in 1854 just before Richardson arrived in Cambridge. He had later studied architecture in the New York atelier established by Richard Morris Hunt when Hunt returned from Paris in the mid-fifties. In the Gambrill and Richardson office the men shared draftsmen and credit for the buildings they produced, but they formed no real creative collaboration. In the partnership, Richardson designed, Gambrill managed. The association lasted until 1878, four years after Richardson had moved back to New England. Two years later, for reasons unknown, Gambrill shot himself dead.

In this early period the bulk of Richardson's commissions came from New England and upstate New York. His Harvard ties served him well in both areas. Through Rumrill and his father-in-law he quickly received other commissions in Springfield, Massachusetts. While he was working on the Western Railroad offices there in 1867, Julia reported to her mother that she thought he was going crazy, "for he had a headache & kept talking in his sleep about the staircase." And he early worked in and around Boston. Benjamin Crowninshield, whose private journal of his student days at Harvard told us so much about Richardson's undergraduate life, commissioned a four-story town house for the city's posh Back Bay section.

Charles Learoyd also shows up frequently in Crowninshield's journal. He had become rector of Grace Church in Medford, Massachusetts, in 1866 and the next year invited Richardson to enter a limited competition for the design of a new church, perhaps with the concurrence of local Harvardians Josiah Bradlee and Shepherd Brooks. Bradlee we remember from Paris; Brooks and his family

Office of H. H. Richardson, rendering of an unexecuted design for a Civil War Memorial for Worcester, Massachusetts, 1868. Although a native of New Orleans, Richardson designed a number of postwar monuments to the Union cause. (Printing and Graphic Arts, Houghton Library, Harvard University, Cambridge, Massachusetts)

were among the area's richest folks and became major donors to the building fund. In a letter to the architect acknowledging receipt of his drawings, Rev. Learoyd reported that the committee unanimously agreed that "there was more genius and originality in them" than in any others that had come before it. For his part, he admitted that Richardson's design had given him "a distaste for all others." High praise for the young architect's work, but Harvard old-boy preference shines forth here, for the one surviving drawing of the church by another architect shows a project rather similar to Richardson's.

Despite Rev. Learoyd's accolades, Richardson also heard what was to become a refrain in his career: the project seemed vastly beyond the church's $25,000 budget. "Committees," Learoyd wrote apologetically, "are an unreasonable set of men—for they want a striking, beautiful and commodious church for a smaller sum of money." He wished Richardson was there in person to convince the committee that he could build his project—so much more impressive than his competitors', what with all that hammered stone in the tower and on the front—for the allotted sum. In the end the committee accepted Richardson's design, although during construction it was repeatedly altered to conform more closely to the budget.

Grace Church still stands. It lacks the front arcade and the Sunday school wing but is otherwise something of a reprise of that at Springfield, except for the glacial bolder walls recommended by the Brookses. These would reappear more significantly in the architect's later work.

OPPOSITE: Exterior detail of Grace Church, Medford, Massachusetts, 1867–69. Richardson began early to work with the weight and tactile quality of the rough-faced granite that was to become his trademark.

Other characteristics of the Medford commission also recur throughout Richardson's career. A pattern had already developed in which his Harvard connections supplied him with work, he designed over budget, the client was apologetic, Richardson talked the committee into building, and the original project needed to be altered in execution. It was a litany of give-and-take, of proposal and persuasion, and when Richardson could interact personally with client or committee, he often had his way. People wanted to please him.

These early years brought another Massachusetts project that, although unrealized, deserves attention. In 1867 the Worcester City Council solicited designs for a memorial to the city's Civil War dead. Gambrill and Richardson submitted a monument designed as a medieval variation on the Arc de Triomphe in Paris, a proposal that, although favored by the committee, proved too expensive and remained unbuilt. Clearly Richardson had quickly put behind him his divided loyalties of the war years. He resurrected this design seven years later for another, similarly unexecuted war monument for Buffalo, and still later it influenced Shepley, Rutan and Coolidge's arch at Stanford University and Stanford White's arch for Washington Square in New York City.

Other than Massachusetts, the bulk of Richardson's early commissions came from upstate New York, where there were also Harvard connections. The most important was William Dorsheimer. The architect's senior by six years, Dorsheimer attended Phillips Andover and Harvard (without graduating) and joined the bar in 1854. During the war he rose to the rank of major on the staff of Gen. John C. Frémont. Entering politics with the resumption of peace, he held a variety of important positions, culminating with that of lieutenant governor of the state from 1874 to 1880 and United States congressman in 1883–85. Like Olmsted and Richardson, he was a member of the Century Association. When he decided to build a house in Buffalo in 1868, the old-boy network provided him with his architect.

The Dorsheimer house takes its cue generally from the *hôtels* of Second Empire Paris and specifically from designs found in Richardson's copy of Victor Petit's *Châteaux de la Vallée de la Loire*. Before its later alteration, a visitor entered through the axial portal in the principal facade on the south, or garden, side to find a central stair hall flanked by echoing parlors. The exterior sports a gray-slate mansard above a gray sandstone frame filled with ocher-colored brick and incised with that debased classical detail known in France as Neo-Grec.

As lieutenant governor of New York, William Dorsheimer would send even more important work to Richardson's office, and eventually the architect's gratitude would inspire him to enter the political fray on Dorsheimer's behalf. All politics is local, according to the popular aphorism, but what politics we hear about from Richardson was personal. He spouted no political (or architectural) theory, but, almost two decades after the building of Dorsheimer's house, he saw an opportunity to help along his friend's career, as we learn from a letter to Olmsted written early in 1885.

Civil Service reform was a major issue in the election of 1884, and a group of independent Republicans called Mugwumps, unhappy with their candidate, James G. Blaine, had helped elect to the presidency the Democratic governor of New York, Grover Cleveland. From Washington Richardson wrote Olmsted concerning candidates for Cleveland's cabinet. There was at hand a contest between William C. Whitney, whom Richardson described as a machine politician, and their old friend Dorsheimer. Reminding Olmsted of "all that he has done for both of us," the architect asked Olmsted to put pressure on the Boston Mugwumps in favor of Dorsheimer. Talk to Charles Sargent, John Quincy Adams, Charles Francis Adams, and Charles Codman, he urged; "now is the time for the men who feel alike . . . to hang together." The Brahmin old-school network governed not only architecture and social life, but politics as well. In this case, however, the wire pulling did not succeed, and in 1885 Dorsheimer retired to the editorial life.

If the churches at Springfield and Medford are mainly English in inspiration, William Dorsheimer's house in Buffalo, like the architect's own house on Staten Island, is thoroughly French. Into the later years of the nineteenth century the bulk of American architecture was inspired by European influences, but after the Civil War a few independent designers began to transform—rather than imitate—these sources of inspiration. Richardson was among the leaders of this movement toward cultural independence, but in the beginning he too found it expedient to follow the tried and true path.

American architecture of the middle of the nineteenth century took its lead from Europe in general and England and France in particular. English architecture of the period was picturesque, polychromatic, eclectic, and based largely on Gothic forms, especially those of northern Italy. French architecture continued to follow the gray-limestone and blue-slate classicism that had become a national trait in the Renaissance and was codified by the Académie and the École. In the pluralistic United States, however, these styles carried no specific nationalistic meaning, and so it was possible to combine them.

Associationism was a ruling dictum, and it insisted that certain architectural forms and styles were appropriate for some types of building, other styles appropriate for others. A Christian church demanded Gothic, for example; a bank or urban office building, French classical or Italian design. A young architect wins his first commissions by satisfying such expectations on the part of his clients, so Richardson's early buildings oscillate between the prevailing tendencies of his day, between the English Gothic of the Springfield and Medford churches and the French mansard of his own house and Dorsheimer's. This following of fashion would not last, however, for he soon developed his own voice, and called others to follow *his* lead.

The years 1869–71 formed a period of transition, as Richardson settled into a successful architectural practice in which he began tentatively to assert his own individuality. The crisis of his Anglo-French phase came with his design for the high school at Worcester. Gambrill and Richardson won a limited competition for the building in 1869, a competition they were probably invited into on the strength of their earlier project for a war memorial. Richardson's training at the École produced an effective plan, a rational resolution to the complex building program. His exterior, however—a picturesque concoction of English polychromy and an anorexic main tower that shot well above the roof to splinter against the sky, all weakly constrained by French axes, corner pavilions, and mansard roof—proved as gawky as a first-growth teenager. The building's destruction some years ago meant no loss to America's cultural heritage.

If Richardson seemed to grow bored with expected modes of current architectural design at the Worcester High School, his next major project showed him setting off in a new direction. In 1869, Boston's Brattle Square Congregational Church decided to move from its dilapidated downtown building to a prominent site on Commonwealth Avenue, in the new Back Bay section of the city. Benjamin Crowninshield, father of that Harvard chum who had already commissioned a Back Bay house from the architect, was a major supporter of the move, and through that now familiar linkage, Gambrill and Richardson were invited to a limited competition, which they won. The T-shaped interior was never finished according to Richardson's wishes and was never a success, but the exterior is. Roxbury pudding-stone walls are trimmed with dark red sandstone; the main arcade and the openings in the tower are round arches composed of voussoirs of alternating colors. The church presents a stony quietude that is new in the architect's work but would soon become another signature characteristic.

Brattle Square Church's chief glory, however, resides in the sturdy tower at the corner of Commonwealth and Clarendon Streets. We need only glance back at the spike impaling the Worcester High School to measure the leap Richardson has accomplished in such a short time. Here its chief feature is a high-relief frieze beneath the crowning machicolations, executed by a thirty-seven-year-old Frenchman named Auguste Bartholdi, whom Richardson met in the studio of the painter John La Farge. Bartholdi was touring the United States in 1870, promoting his idea for a monument to Franco-American friendship, a monument that eventually became the Statue of Liberty in New York Harbor. For the Brattle Square congregation he represented four Christian rites: baptism, Communion, marriage, and burial. It was said that among the figures are portraits of Richardson, La Farge, and even Lincoln. At the corners stand angels of judgment holding long gilt trumpets, their silhouettes against the sky early giving the church its popular nickname of the "Holy Beanblowers."

The unsatisfactory acoustics within Brattle Square Church and the bank-

ruptcy of the congregation in 1876 led to calls for the building's demolition, but no one ever suggested removing the tower. It was said, in fact, to be protected in perpetual trust by a memorial society. Almost universally admired, it earned Richardson his first notice in the national press. In 1875 *Appleton's Journal* praised him for making the tower the distinguishing feature rather than "breaking the mass of the church with petty details"—this was cogent recognition of Richardson's new direction as he began to seek cohesion, rather than the dispersion his contemporaries sought, in building design. A fresh form in the architecture of the time, Brattle Square tower briefly became Richardson's best advertisement. It attracted the attention of a broad spectrum of influential and potentially important people, including the Cambridge poet and Harvard professor James Russell Lowell, and a budding architect of the next generation named Louis Henry Sullivan.

Around the back of the church, overlooking a service alley dotted with trash cans, Richardson used molded iron columns to support a broad horizontal opening in the stone exterior—a use of iron that would draw much attention in the

Main front of the Brattle Square Church, Boston, 1869–73. In the design of this early church, Richardson began to find his own direction in the use of round-arched granite forms.

Exterior detail, Trinity Church Parsonage (with the tower of Brattle Square Church in the background), Boston, 1879–80. Richardson specified old-fashioned carved-brick ornament on this and similar exteriors rather than the terra-cotta commonly used by his contemporaries.

H. H. Richardson, Hampden County Courthouse, Springfield, Massachusetts, 1871–74. The Romanesque details, sturdy random ashlar masonry, and asymmetrical placement of the balcony in an otherwise symmetrical facade are all Richardsonian signatures.

twentieth century. During the nineteenth century, architecture changed from a system of load-bearing natural materials to a lightweight expression of man-made products. Iron, steel, and plate glass gradually infiltrated or completely replaced stone, brick, and wood. Some architects adhered to traditional techniques and traditional forms, others embraced new techniques but continued to design in traditional forms, and still others sought a new architectural expression using the new structural materials and techniques. To some twentieth-century critics, who saw Richardson as a precursor of "modern" architecture, his use of iron in the window at the rear of Brattle Square Church revealed the architect embracing the products of the Industrial Revolution. But this window overlooks a back alley, not Commonwealth Avenue. This use of exposed iron is very rare in his work, and it is here, as usual, deemphasized rather than celebrated. When he incorporated iron structurally in his buildings, as he apparently did much later at the Marshall Field Wholesale Store, he usually concealed it. For Richardson architecture was a matter of traditional natural materials used in traditional ways, although he would adopt those traditions to his own formal ends and to building programs developed in his own time.

If in the design of Brattle Square Church Richardson began to pull away from the Anglo-French references of his earlier works, his 1871 Hampden County Courthouse in Springfield, Massachusetts, marks another tentative step along his new path. With an I-shaped plan following the principles of the Parisian École and a tower that descends from medieval Italy, the design continued to draw important characteristics from Europe, but its monochromatic exterior of rough-faced gray Monson granite ashlar trimmed with polished stones and its central entrance of triple round-arched openings anticipate the breadth and quietude of his later work. A corner balcony, reflecting the building's location at the angle of the main civic square, is an unbalanced element in an otherwise symmetrical facade, another new feature. This interplay between symmetry and asymmetry was to become a characteristic compositional device. The building, the design commission for which he won in a competition, survives significantly altered.

The steady stream of work that quickly entered the office could not be handled by Gambrill and Richardson alone, and they began to introduce help into the drafting rooms at 6 Hanover Street and then 57 Broadway. The Broadway workplace occupied a typically narrow, cast-iron-fronted commercial building facing Exchange Place, just to the south of Richard Upjohn's famed Gothic Revival Trinity Church at the head of Wall Street. It preserved the ideas of an earlier generation, but it served well as the home not only of the firm of Gambrill and Richardson but later of the famous partnership of McKim, Mead and White. Charles Follen McKim and Stanford White had in fact both cut their architectural teeth with Gambrill and Richardson when the partners were still at 6 Hanover Street. Despite McKim and White's long association, they were diametrically opposed individuals. McKim, taciturn, cerebral, and stiff, had left Harvard for Europe to travel and study at the École in Paris, and as a twenty-three-year-old joined Richardson as his chief assistant in May 1870. White, a gifted draftsman with no training whatsoever, entered the office at age sixteen later that summer on the recommendation of Frederick Law Olmsted. He was an energetic, intuitive, and brilliant redhead. They joined, among others, T. M. Clark, an expert on technology who later published a manual on building superintendence, and Charles H. Rutan. The latter, two years White's senior, had come into the firm the previous year as an office boy, grew into an indispensable engineer, and was one of the three principals to whom the dying Richardson would leave his practice.

Not all the architect's work in this period was ecclesiastical or civic. The postwar era saw the dawning of new domestic design that would by the 1880s produce the great seaside and suburban wooden houses that have come to be called the American Shingle style. During the New York years Gambrill and Richardson turned out a triad of domestic buildings, two of which were executed, that mark the beginning of this development, in that they combine English planning and style with American materials. They were the first steps in the direction of Richardson's fully realized Shingle style houses of his later years.

The earliest of these houses was a project for a Harvardian and Porcellian who was four years Richardson's junior and a friend of his wife's family. In 1868 Richard Codman asked Richardson to design a house for a site in West Roxbury, near Boston. In his memoirs Codman recounted that he paid for the finished plans, canceled the project, and had "all the fun of building without having to pay for it." What Richardson thought of that is mercifully unrecorded, although the two did remain friends. Surviving drawings show that the first floor was to have been centered on a "living hall" containing entrance, fireplace, and staircase. The English origins of this hall were echoed in the hooded roofs, half timbering, and leaded casement windows of the exterior.

Four years later the architect began work on the 1872 F. W. Andrews summerhouse at Newport. The project may have come into the firm through Gambrill, but the route as usual ran through Harvard, for Frank Andrews graduated from the Cambridge college the year before Richardson's partner. Larger than the Codman project (and long ago destroyed by fire), the house had a living hall that occupied the center of the main floor, surrounded by porches. The spiky outline—all roof, gables, dormers, and chimneys— capped exterior walls that were partly covered with clapboards and partly with shingles. The wood shingles, new to American domestic building in this work, were a variation on the tilework of contemporary English Queen Anne design, especially that of Richard Norman Shaw, and they would soon become the dominant external cladding for American seaside cottages and suburban homes.

This series of early domestic designs culminated in the 1874 William Watts Sherman summerhouse at Newport, a commission that probably came to the firm on the strength of the Andrews house. Sherman, a trained physician and practicing banker, was married to Annie Derby Rogers Whetmore, daughter of a prominent New York merchant family and sister of George P. Whetmore, later governor of Rhode Island and United States senator. George Whetmore lived next door, at Château-sur-Mer, a masterpiece of Francophile design by Richard Morris Hunt, but for Wetmore's sister Richardson adapted English forms to American materials. The house exists, but it was later enlarged and the interiors altered. Drawings for the original interiors, however, point to old English sources. They also display the gifted hand of Stanford White, then in his early twenties, who developed in the office of Gambrill and Richardson into a nimble draftsman and clever decorator, whose talents become increasingly evident in the 1870s.

Richardson's plan arranged the Sherman house rooms asymmetrically around the living hall. The exterior rises into an Anglo-picturesque pile of roof, gables, and chimneys covered with shingles, half timbering, multipaned windows, and decorative accents. There is also the suggestion of a horizontal layering of exterior elements, a compositional device that will become an important characteristic of Richardson's mature work. The Codman project and the Andrews and Sherman houses, like Richardson's other work of this formative period, show the

Exterior of the William Watts Sherman house, Newport, Rhode Island, 1874–75. This rich composition of shingles, half-timbering, stucco, and glass closely followed the contemporary work of the English architect Richard Norman Shaw, but Richardson was soon to abandon this direction.

architect struggling to achieve his own design vocabulary by adapting European methods to American needs and materials.

Richardson kept the office busy during these years with an ongoing and very large commission for the Buffalo State Hospital for the Insane. In 1869 Gov. John Hoffman appointed a building committee that included several of Richardson's friends and former clients, including William Dorsheimer. He got the job and brought in Frederick Law Olmsted as landscape architect. Construction stretched over the decade, providing office chores and revenue during the severe economic depression of the mid-seventies, caused by the failure of the banking house of Jay Cooke and Company.

Proper housing and treatment for the mentally ill preoccupied many people in the middle of the nineteenth century, with the prevailing theory suggesting that improper behavior caused by an unregulated life in an unsuitable environment produced insanity. A leading doctor, Thomas S. Kirkbride of the Pennsylvania Hospital for the Insane, published a book on asylum architecture in 1854, illustrated with the designs of the Philadelphia architect Samuel Sloan. There he insisted on a highly regulated life for inmates, who were to be separated into semidetached buildings arranged in echelon. The Kirkbride plan controlled asylum architecture for the next generation.

John Gray, the director of the Buffalo asylum, expected Richardson to follow the Kirkbride-Sloan model, an expectation that was in fact perfectly compatible with the axial, hierarchial parti he had learned to design at the École. His overall inspiration was medieval and French. Individual well-lighted and well-ventilated pavilions connected by quadrant passages form a broad V in plan, with the administrative block at its apex marked by twin towers. The exterior sandstone is laid in random ashlar pattern (although to save money this became brick on the outer pavilions). The hospital remains one of Richardson's largest commissions, but in part because it depends so heavily upon the ideas of others, it has never been ranked among his greatest works.

During Richardson's first years as a professional architect, his work was marked by his educational experiences in France and his knowledge of building in England. He drew upon his library to refresh his memory of European architecture. Increasingly, however, he moved away from a close reliance on such sources as he began to use local materials, round-arched details, a minimum of color contrast, and quieter forms to create a distinctly personal style. In his New York years his achievement was tentative, but he did establish a basis for the extraordinarily original works of the coming years.

Between 1869 and 1876 Richardson recorded his design ideas in a large sketchbook in which he also jotted personal memos. As he lay indisposed on September 30, 1872, the day after his thirty-fourth birthday as well as the day of birth of his fourth child and second son, Henry Hyslop, he made out a list of clothes for his older son, John Cole Hayden, as if he were ordering the three-year-old's wardrobe from Poole's. He listed a suit, including jacket, waistcoat, and kilt, an overcoat, and some white shirts. He also pondered his growing family: next to his and Julia's initials he jotted down the childrens'. The sons came first, although second and fourth in order of birth; the daughters came next, although first and third. The gendered pecking order reflected characteristically Victorian ideas.

These familial musings appear on a page that includes several unfinished sketches for an unidentified house. Was Richardson contemplating larger quarters for his growing brood? And where might that house be located? In the period between November 1866 and the spring of 1874 he designed some forty-four buildings and projects, fewer than ten of which were located in New York City (and many of these were minor alterations). Since his commissions came from north and east of the city, he had avoided serious contact with the building mania in his own front yard. Four months earlier, in June, he had won the competition for the design of Trinity Church in Boston. It must have been increasingly clear to him that it would soon be time to end his New York exile. Much of his work had been in New England, his client base resided there, and he had now to supervise in Boston one of the most important architectural commissions in the country. By June 1874 Richardson had moved his practice and his family to Brookline, near Boston. The office of Gambrill and Richardson in New York remained open for a few more years, but Richardson's total attention was now focused on his early masterpiece, Trinity Church on Copley Square.

6 ❖ TRINITY CHURCH 1872–77

RICHARDSON LAID THE CORNERSTONE OF HIS CAREER WITH THE winning design for Trinity Church on Copley Square in Boston's Back Bay. With this work he became the Richardson of historical stature. On the personal level it placed him, at age thirty-three and just six and a half years after his return from Paris, at the top of his profession in the United States, and made him a figure of international renown. Along with literature such as Mark Twain's *Tom Sawyer* and the hidden poetry of Emily Dickinson, paintings such as Thomas Eakins's contemporary *Gross Clinic* and Winslow Homer's *Breezing Up!*, and works of similar eminence in other arts, on another level Trinity represented the coming of age of the "American generation," that group of artists born in or near the 1830s who emerged in the wake of the Civil War and who created a distinctly American culture at the time of the nation's centennial. They no longer blindly followed European precedent but adapted it to American needs and wants. The design and erection of Trinity formed a central event in Richardson's professional life; it remains a central monument in America's cultural heritage.

Trinity Church still dominates Copley Square. The upstart John Hancock Building and Weston Hotel tower above it, but they seem too frail to challenge its authority. The Copley Plaza Hotel, Boston Public Library, and New Old South Church make worthy neighbors, but they merely form the frame for its majestic presence. Trinity reigns physically, historically, and artistically.

As with all of Richardson's best designs, Trinity is the product of teamwork. It incorporates the contributions of a host of well-known collaborators, among them Charles McKim, Stanford White, O. W. Norcross, John La Farge, Augustus Saint-Gaudens, William Morris, and Edward Burne-Jones. All labored to create a house suitable for the ministry of the Reverend Phillips Brooks, whose likeness appears no less than four times inside the church and out. All were controlled by the genius of H. H. Richardson, who is honored for "his noblest work" by a memorial from his professional peers on a wall of the cloister. That memorial reminds many of Sir Christopher Wren's at St. Paul's in London, which instructs the visitor seeking the architect's monument to look at the building itself.

In its design Trinity resulted primarily from a collaboration between Richardson and Brooks, and during its construction they became fast friends. Born in 1835 of the meeting of two prominent New England families, Phillips Brooks

graduated from the Boston Latin School then entered Harvard, "according to the custom of his ancestors," with the class of 1855. During the decade of his ministry at fashionable Holy Trinity Church on Rittenhouse Square in Philadelphia—a building designed by John Notman in the Romanesque style—he established his reputation as a spellbinding preacher. He spoke to the "breathless multitudes" who crowded Holy Trinity Sunday after Sunday, unable to resist his "witchery," according to one observer. After Boston called Brooks to become the rector of Trinity, in the middle of 1869, he continued to impress. The Word, housed in Brooks's commanding figure and expressed through his shining eyes and resonant voice, occupied the center of any service at which he presided, and it became the raison d'être of Richardson's design.

With Trinity as his base, Brooks became one of the most famous clerics of the era. He would remain rector of the church until 1891, and then assume the office of Episcopal bishop of Massachusetts. (Among his more popular accomplishments was the writing of the Christmas hymn "O Little Town of Bethlehem.")

Cloister, chancel, and tower of Trinity Church, Copley Square, Boston, 1872–77. Trinity represents the coming of age of American culture at the time of the nation's centennial.

When as the new rector he first preached in Boston, in October 1869, Trinity was housed in a fine example of Boston Granite Gothic building that stood on Summer Street near Washington. In less than a year, however, under Brooks's guiding ambition, the decision had been made to follow the shift in residential population out of the old center and into the new and upscale Back Bay area. By the time old Trinity burned in Boston's Great Fire of November 1872, plans were well advanced for its replacement. By late 1871 the parish had purchased land where the church now stands and selected a building committee headed by the architect George M. Dexter and including a representative selection of Brahmin Boston: Charles H. Parker, Robert C. Winthrop, Martin Brimmer, Charles R. Codman, John C. Ropes, John G. Cushing, and Charles D. Morrill. Robert Treat Paine, capitalist, descendant of a signer of the Declaration of Independence, graduate of Harvard in Phillips Brooks's class, and later client for one of Richardson's finest country houses, assumed the chair at Dexter's untimely death just after he had announced the results of the competition.

On March 12, 1872, the committee invited six architectural firms by letter to a limited competition for the commission. The list included Ware and Van Brunt, then building Harvard's Memorial Hall; Peabody and Stearns; William A. Potter, then at work on the local post office; John Sturgis, then engaged at the Museum of Fine Arts, adjacent to the site of the intended church; Richard Morris

H. H. Richardson, first sketches for Trinity Church, Boston, 1872. These "ideograms" were drawn on the back of the letter requesting the architect to compete for the design of the Rev. Phillips Brooks's new church. (Printing and Graphic Arts, Houghton Library, Harvard University, Cambridge, Massachusetts)

Hunt, then busy with the Lenox Library in New York; and H. H. Richardson. Above all else the program called for an auditorium, a vessel in which to carry Brooks's voice. The letter requested designs for the erection of a church to seat 1,350 people on the main floor and in galleries. There were to be no columns, and "good acoustic qualities" were important. ("No obtrusive columns to impede the preacher's power," according to a dedicatory sermon five years later.) Drawings were due by the first of May.

When Richardson received the letter at his drafting rooms at 57 Broadway in New York, he turned it over and proceeded to treat the request like a design program at the École, quickly sketching his first thoughts on the reverse with a pencil. These are ideograms for alternative spatial types, one with long nave, narrow side aisles, with or without a clerestory, and the other a Greek cross in plan. On further reflection about the proscription against columns, which would be necessary in a church divided into nave and aisles, he opted for the modified Greek cross as the more suitable to the demands of a preaching hall.

These are precious documents. Here we witness the original act of architectural creation. In these marks we watch Richardson give shape to his most celebrated work. We can see the moment of conception, the fertilized seed of the great church that was to rise in the heart of the Back Bay. Through all subsequent changes—and there were many, and they were significant—the basic schema jotted down on the back of the letter remained the guiding idea of the design. One of his friends recalled that he "had a rare intuitive sense that enabled him to strike

at the foundation and grasp the whole of a truth at once." He learned the process in Paris, and it remained fundamental to Richardson's method throughout his life. It resulted in buildings that were disciplined, graspable, powerful, and memorable.

Once the overall form of the building had been established by Richardson through a further series of ideograms, as was typical the office force of five assistants began to generate scale drawings. In his maturity the architect seldom drew after the first sketches established the direction of a design, although he would criticize the graphic work of his helpers. He made a distinction between a good draftsman and an architect; patience could make the former, not the latter. It must have been a very busy time at 57 Broadway. The office then had in hand four major projects as well as other miscellaneous work, and there were only six weeks in which to develop Richardson's initial impulse, criticize it, then produce the definitive plan, three elevations, longitudinal and cross sections, and perspective called for by the terms of the competition. Historians usually credit McKim as draftsman of the presentation drawings, although when McKim left the office shortly after the winner was announced, fiery Stanford White—then all of eighteen years old—became Richardson's man on the job.

The day he heard he had won the commission, in the first week of June 1872, Richardson, a roll of drawings in hand, burst in on his Staten Island neighbors and interrupted their breakfast with shouts of "I've got it! I've got it! I've got it! I've got the Church—Trinity Church—in Boston." He then bolted out the door and back to his delighted family. He had already wired Dexter his thanks for the good news. He had prevailed over his competitors, most of whom were better established in the profession and some of whom also had Harvard connections, to grasp the architectural plum. He had every reason to be satisfied, proud, and thrilled.

In the midst of triumph there was a note of foreboding, however. Richardson's energetic response to the good news must be set against notices of his physical ill-being. Up to this moment in the architect's life we have heard little about his health. As a youth he had been fit and athletic, but that now began to change. It gradually became apparent in the 1870s that he was as flawed in body

LEFT: *Office of H. H. Richardson, competition perspective for Trinity Church, Boston, 1872, preserved in a photograph of the lost drawing. Richardson's winning design was later modified by reducing the height and changing the design of the tower. (Printing and Graphic Arts, Houghton Library, Harvard University, Cambridge, Massachusetts)*

RIGHT: *H. H. Richardson, preliminary plan for Trinity Church, Boston, 1872. The architect's bold graphic style carried into what he called his "bold, living architecture." (Printing and Graphic Arts, Houghton Library, Harvard University, Cambridge, Massachusetts)*

as he was gifted in imagination. References to sickness riddle his correspondence from early in his career, and one draft of Robert Treat Paine's report of the Trinity Church building committee noted that nothing happened immediately after Richardson won the commission because of his "long & serious illness during the summer & autumn" of 1872. Paine and John Ropes were dispatched from Boston to New York to interview the architect at the end of the year to learn whether he could "be depended upon, in the state of his health."

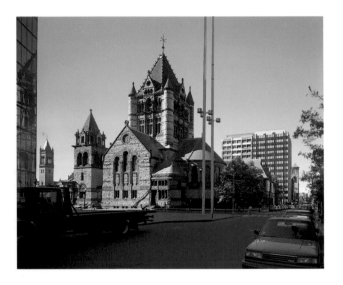

Exterior flank of Trinity Church, Copley Square, Boston, 1872–77. Trinity's central tower dominates and unifies the pyramidal exterior composition.

In an undated note to another member of the building committee, Charles Parker, Richardson explained that he had for many years been the victim of a "very bad" hernia, had broken his truss, and was obliged to keep quiet until it could be fixed. If these early reports of ill health referred only to a hernia, the situation probably caused him more hindrance to his movements than threat to his life, although that hindrance was to cause him serious problems for the remainder of his days. In 1879 he was again sent to bed for three months because of it. The opposition of energy and ailment that first surfaces here will become a governing aspect of his remaining years.

Richardson drew his winning design for Trinity Church for a rectangular lot on the east side of what was to become Copley Square. It grouped a broad nave, transepts, and chancel around a tall awkward tower rising above the crossing. The parish house called for in the program sat to the east of the main edifice. The church in these drawings is Romanesque, and the interior was to have had a colorful decorative pattern, but the overall scheme looked awkward. The composition as a whole appeared disjointed. In fact critics have often wondered how Richardson won the competition with such a gawky design; certainly his first project was not measurably better than several of those that lost.

We do not know specifically what swung the committee in his favor, but the vote of one member, Charles Codman, permits something of a glimpse into the discussion. Although the letter requesting competitive designs stipulated that they were to be anonymous, signed only with a cipher, Codman had no trouble identifying individual architects. He favored only two of the projects, those of John Sturgis and H. H. Richardson, and of the two he very much preferred the former. Its interior, he thought, was "remarkably beautiful & much better than Mr. Richardson's," while the exteriors were about equal. The cost (of course) and the weight of the structure also worried him in Richardson's design. The rest of the committee may have reflected on Codman's bias as Sturgis's brother-in-law when they voted to give his second choice the prize.

The parish saved Richardson from building his original concept because it almost immediately added a triangular piece of land to its original plot, and the drawings had to be revised as soon as he was physically able. What's more, the building was to be erected on the filled land of the Back Bay, using as its underpinnings some forty-four hundred oak piles driven into the muck, and that realization gave rise to further design changes. Such a site recalled the delta fill of Richardson's native New Orleans. The engineers eventually decided that the weight of the high tower as originally conceived could not be sustained by such a foundation, and a lighter and squatter profile resulted. The redesign moved the parish house to the north, onto the new triangle, and incorporated a lower central tower. With any number of major and minor adjustments, these revisions produced the building dedicated in February 1877.

Negotiations over design revisions during 1873 and 1874 meant frequent trips between New York and Boston on the part of Richardson and Stanford White. Long hours on the train were followed by even longer hours in meetings with the committee, the engineers, or the builder. Details had to be fixed, fees established, materials selected, disagreements ironed out. All of this taxed when it did not bore. According to White's letters home, he and the boss rewarded themselves on these trips by eating and drinking, "unteetotal-like," with gusto. White drank champagne with his supper, but Richardson, he reported, consumed "brandies, gins, wines and cigars" with his boiled tripe, or, as the architect described the dish, the "entrails of a Cow." The reminiscences of the architect's associates reiterate accounts of such eating habits. Richardson's unspecified ailment of 1872 seems to have subsided, but it is no wonder that he occasionally complained of being indisposed or that he encountered serious digestive problems within a few years of finishing the church.

In its execution Trinity was a collaboration between Richardson and O. W. Norcross. An architect requires a builder to realize his design; the reputation of the designer is in the hands of the executor. Richardson had the wisdom early in his career to attach to himself a contractor of extraordinary ability. As early as the Worcester High School, he had worked with Orlando Whitney Norcross of Norcross Brothers, Contractors and Builders of Worcester, Massachusetts, who were to construct the bulk of his remaining buildings. A self-taught engineer one year younger than Richardson, O. W. rose to become the most important general contractor in the country, eventually erecting buildings across the United States for

Detail of the exterior of Trinity Church, Copley Square, Boston, 1872–77. Richardson's designs changed during construction as he tested his drawings amid the lights and shadows of reality.

architects such as McKim, Mead and White; Peabody and Stearns; Shepley, Rutan and Coolidge; and John Russell Pope, among many others.

According to one authority, Norcross possessed a "superior practical knowledge of all that pertains to building." Although his work for Richardson was generally conservative, after the architect's death he flowered into an innovative technician, with numerous patented building processes to his credit, including one for reinforced concrete flat-slab construction. H. H. and O. W. not only became "great business associates" but "strong personal friends" as well, and this despite the fact that they were very different people. Norcross was a "short, sturdy, dark complexioned man, with snapping brown eyes" whose walrus mustache drooped beneath a prominent nose. A veteran of the Union army and a teetotaler to boot, he seemed "quick thinking, quick speaking, determined," according to John J. Glessner, whose Richardson-designed Chicago house he was to build. Richardson and Norcross nonetheless usually saw eye to eye when it came to erecting buildings.

From Trinity Church onward, O. W. became Richardson's master builder. The architect had in his office two employees skilled in engineering and building technology, Charles Rutan and T. M. Clark. He nonetheless introduced Norcross to the design process at its very beginning, in part because of the quality of his work, in part because Norcross owned the quarries and the mills that would eventually supply the building materials, in part because he could accurately estimate building costs (which, frequently, the architect ignored). Although some members of Richardson's staff were not happy with the arrangement, thinking that the architect ought to be in charge of everything, Norcross can be considered Richardson's collaborator in the process of making buildings.

This applied even to correcting drawings and altering details when they seemed inadequate for the job at hand. Glenn Brown, who worked as a carpenter at Trinity after some architectural training and eventually became the national secretary of the American Institute of Architects, often redrafted details during the time he worked as Norcross's clerk of the works. In the process he "became very familiar with the drawings from Richardson's office—was much impressed with their artistic qualities and wondered at his ability in ignoring practical considerations." Richardson could afford to be less than specific. He knew he had in Norcross a practical extension of his own intentions. Besides, the architect considered himself only loosely bound by his builder's estimates of cost.

Richardson had in general a cavalier attitude toward builders. "Architects," he wrote in an 1870 memo to himself, "should not be made the convenience of contractors," and they should not press him for drawings. Norcross often complained during the building of Trinity that the lack of drawings from the architect's office caused delays and raised costs. Nor does there seem to have been complete harmony between architect, builder, and building committee (represented by Robert Treat Paine). Trinity Church Archives hold many a letter from one or the other of these men dealing with lack of information, delays, and unforeseen added costs, and hinting at personal animosity during construction. Paine's interference at the building site angered Norcross; Richardson's reluctance to provide specific information about weights and measures to the building committee, aggravated by his supplying incorrect estimates about the weight of the main tower, irritated Paine; Norcross's tardiness with cost estimates rankled the committee and Richardson. There was hesitation all around about committing to specific numbers too quickly.

The Trinity building committee got on the architect's nerves. They were working with "devotion & energy," he admitted to Brooks in October 1874, but with "perhaps a sprinkle of the Star Chamber." In this reference he drew upon his undergraduate reading of Macauley's *History of England* to recall the secret, oppressive, and arbitrary judicial body that held sway in sixteenth-century England. Red tape complicated matters, as did an "apparently total want of confidence in everybody." The committee's influence dampened enthusiasm all around, for the members meant well but did not understand their responsibility. Richardson had not yet perfected his ability to mold clients to his wishes.

Anyone who has ever built anything, even remodeled a kitchen, will understand that any building campaign causes strains among the principals. A large project magnifies the problems; a self-assertive architect compounds them. These were all capable men, however, and conflict seems eventually to have brought out the best in each of them. Despite the battles of the moment, Trinity emerged as a masterpiece, Paine hired Richardson for later work, and Norcross went on to build again and again for the architect.

At the time of Trinity Church's dedication, Richardson provided a description that clearly stated his stylistic references in the building. He saw it as "a free rendering of the French Romanesque," and particularly that of the region of the Auvergne. There is no evidence that Richardson traveled to central France during his student days, although he did later, so his knowledge of this architecture necessarily derived from his library. In the Auvergne, in the ecclesiastical architecture of the twelfth century, wrote Richardson, "the tower became, as it were, the Church, and the composition took the outline of a pyramid, the apse, transepts, nave and chapels forming only the base to the obelisk of the tower." This

Exterior detail, Trinity Church Parish house, Boston, 1872–75. At Trinity, the architect began to reduce architectural design to essential elements such as solid and void enriched with constrained ornamental details.

choice perfectly suited Trinity's free-standing site and the auditorium plan required by the building program.

"Instead of the tower being an inconvenient and unnecessary addition to the Church," the architect went on, "it was itself made the main feature. The struggle for precedence, which often takes place between a Church and its spire, was disposed of, by at once and completely subordinating nave, transepts, and apse, and grouping them about the tower as the central mass." Rather than reiterate the asymmetrical, splintered three-dimensional forms so common to the dynamically shaped churches of his contemporaries, as exemplified by Cummings and Sears's New Old South Church, then rising on a corner diagonally across Copley Square, Richardson drew upon the symmetrical and hierarchical format of the École, and perhaps specifically the Prix de Rome project of his friend Julien Guadet. Rather than multiplex, Trinity is uniform. In one stroke Richardson created a church markedly different from that of his peers.

Trinity differed from contemporary work not only in plan and silhouette but in articulation and detail as well. New Old South Church is more characteristic of Victorian architecture: a polychromatic, picturesque pile, Venetian Gothic in detail and richly ornamented with carved, cast, and incised decoration. Its external pointed arches are composed of voussoirs of alternating color to emphasize the individual units of construction. Richardson's choice of the Romanesque produced round-arched openings. His choice of just two colors created by two stones —quarry-faced Dedham granite ashlar for the walls and East Longmeadow sandstone for monochromatic arches and other trim—emphasized the larger aspects of the composition and achieved the "grandeur and repose" he admired in the churches of the Auvergne without slavishly copying them.

In fact the Auvergne provided only one source of inspiration for Trinity. Following that lead, Richardson at first drew an extremely tall tower, but even Charles Codman had worried about its weight, and it had been quickly vetoed by the engineers, who were concerned with its stability on the Back Bay fill. Trinity's crowning glory is lower and broader than called for in the competition drawings. Its source is a Spanish Romanesque model: it was adapted by Stanford White from a cupola on the old cathedral at Salamanca, as depicted in an engraving in the architect's copy of George E. Street's *Gothic Architecture in Spain* of 1865.

Such eclecticism characterized the era. What was new in Richardson's work was the emphasis upon unity rather than diversity in the handling of the disparate parts. The pastor, leaders, and members of the congregation of Trinity Church were all deeply rooted in New England tradition. The Romanesque was exactly the right historical style in which to achieve a fresh but not radical architectural embodiment of their conservatism. This bolder, more primitive style was associated with ecclesiastical architecture but not limited to that reference as was the Gothic favored by most of Richardson's contemporaries. Its characteristics in-

cluded round arches, sturdy piers, massive walls, large forms, restricted ornament, and relatively simple silhouettes when compared to the apparently delicate,
glassy, pointed, and splintered features of the Gothic. It stemmed from the Middle
Ages, and thus suited the needs of a designer who leaned toward pre-Renaissance
and preindustrial forms. The Romanesque lent itself easily for adoption to the
quiet and massive architecture Richardson wished to build.

The random ashlar stonework—a pattern of squared rough-faced stones of
various sizes set in red mortar—that Richardson used in Trinity's exterior granite walls became characteristic of his earlier work. (Later the ashlars became less
variegated in color and were laid up in horizontal, or layered, tiers.) The architect
took advantage of the fact that the Romanesque is a mural architecture. Unlike
the Gothic, where the wall dissolves into diaphanous sheets, Romanesque buildings depend upon the weight of the masonry mass, the play of light, shadow, and
color patterns upon their walls. That is why Richardson thought little of his
drawings and constantly revised his designs, never trusting them until a building was "in stone, beyond recovery," as he told Van Rensselaer. One look at his
massive ashlar buildings and the viewer knows there was nothing otherworldly

*East elevation, Trinity Church
Parish house, Boston, 1872–75.
Richardson's delight in the interplay of symmetry and asymmetry,
horizontal and vertical, light
and shadow, are all apparent in
this view.*

about the architect or his work. Such heavy materials piled up into solid sculptural forms produced a sense of massive physical presence, of permanence, of timeless monumentality new in American architecture.

This sense of architecture as sculpture, of natural materials carved by light and shadow into "bold, rich" forms radiating a sturdy vitality, captures our attention at Trinity as in all of Richardson's mature work. This too sets Richardson's buildings off from those of his contemporaries. It is something of a puzzle, but certainly testimony to its transcendent quality, that his work never went out of fashion during the twentieth century when lightweight, man-made materials seemed to demand thin, textureless, colorless, and expendable buildings. Some twentieth-century historians even found him to be a precursor to modern architecture, despite the fact that his nearly total rejection of industrial materials and forms produced buildings that were essentially antimodern even in their own period. Precursor to modernism, or antimodern in essence, Richardson's work continues to stand on its own through the sheer quality of its design and execution.

The external form of Trinity Church facing Copley Square radiates architectural authority. Its pyramidal outline is profound and powerful. But we are reminded by the more delicate voice of Richardson's slightly older Massachusetts contemporary, the reclusive poet Emily Dickinson, that "the Outer—from the Inner/Derives its Magnitude." Richardson's shaping of Trinity's interior as a pyramidal space gives the exterior its majestic presence, and his decorative treatment of that space gives Trinity its greatest impact.

In its interior decoration Trinity was a collaboration between Richardson and artist John La Farge, La Farge's assistants, and various other glass designers. Richardson's competition drawings depicted a colorful geometrical and figural decorative scheme for the interior, probably again following the lead of the church Guadet included in his Rome Prize–winning project for an Alpine hospice. Richardson sought from the beginning of the project the "rich effect of color in the interior," and he looked to La Farge to achieve this for him. He had to fight the building committee for money and time, but he eventually won the day. La Farge, one year older than Richardson, had studied law and then painting in France and England. He lacked experience in large-scale architectural decoration when Richardson enlisted him for the work at Trinity. In fact, such work was largely unknown in the United States, and Trinity became the first comprehensive, monumental decorative program in the country executed by American artists. What's more, La Farge and his assistants had just five months to complete the project. What they achieved was heroic, a series of huge biblical figures and rich ornamental details set against a deep red background.

It is not so much in its artistic details—although they are indeed fine—as in its overall architectural impact that La Farge's work adds to Richardson's Trinity. In the end, with La Farge's painted walls, the colorful geometric patterns on the overhead wooden barrel vaults, and the eventual incorporation of stained glass by La Farge, Clayton and Bell, William Morris and Edward Burne-Jones, and other French and English designers, Richardson achieved one of the simplest and yet richest ecclesiastical interiors in the country. As Phillips Brooks delivered his sermon, he could be seen and heard from all parts of the ample hall. As he preached he could look for inspiration to La Farge's *Christ in Majesty* above the western entrance, the translucent figure resplendent against the western light and flanked by lancets of luscious aquamarine glass. This is surely the single most stunning example of glasswork in America.

The interior remains much as when it was dedicated, with the exception of changes in the furniture of the chancel, the later pulpit, and the devastating loss of the original wrought-iron chandelier, or "corona," that once gave scale to the vast interior beneath the tower. Frank Lloyd Wright, quoting Chinese philosophers, spoke of the reality of a vessel as the space within. Certainly the interior is the essence of Trinity. Light streaming through the western lancets and other colored windows, falling upon and reflecting from colorfully painted walls, animates the interior. This broad, serene, hushed room seems physically palpable. There is no void here. Shadow and color suffuse the space, scattering the emptiness, filling the cavity. At the dedication, the *Boston Evening Transcript* accurately recorded a "solidity and grandeur of effect not to be described, but to be seen and felt." Trinity houses one of the calmest and most inspirational sacred spaces in the country, if not the world. Good work for an architect about whom it was said there was "nothing spiritual." But then, it was also said that "architecture was his religion."

Richardson's old schoolmate Henry Adams taught history at Harvard and lived in the Back Bay during the building of Trinity. He took a lively interest in the important project designed by his friend the architect for his cousin the preacher. He probably often visited the work in progress, viewing the stonemasons raising the walls, then watching the team of painters under the direction of another friend, John La Farge, as they limned the interior of the dusty, unheated hall. A few years later, when Richardson's work on the Nicholas Anderson house made the architect a frequent guest at Adams's table in Washington, Adams wrote a novel whose setting was Trinity during this work of decoration. In his pseudonymously published roman à clef *Esther*, of 1884, he was to use the church (although he called it St. John's and located it in New York) as the artistic setting for his discussion of the strained relationship between traditional religion and modern science.

Although Adams the novelist emphasized divergence in *Esther*, Richardson the designer created unity. The erstwhile musician here orchestrated a chorus of voices to achieve a harmonious visual choral. Teamwork, beginning with Brooks's voice and the committee's program, moving into the office with the architect's assistants, extending to the engineers and to Norcross Brothers, and ending with the decorative program and stained glass of artists such as La Farge, Morris, and Burne-Jones, all conducted by Richardson's controlling vision, achieved at Trinity Church on Copley Square a powerful singularity of religious and artistic expression. And so it remains today.

Richardson's first use of the Romanesque style, at Trinity Church, echoed across the country in imitations known as the Richardsonian Romanesque, although his own subsequent work often played down its overtly historical features in favor of more elemental architectural values such as superb detailing, controlled silhouette, a studied relationship between open and closed forms, and a relatively restricted palette of natural materials. Almost every major and many a minor city has or has had a Richardsonian Romanesque church with centralized plan and dominant, squat tower, including Philadelphia, Pittsburgh, Detroit, St. Louis, and Kansas City among other places, especially in the Midwest. But not all these admiring offspring were ecclesiastical. Richardson's powerful work lent itself to other building types as well, from courthouses to market halls. Trinity Church joined Richardson's later Allegheny County Courthouse, in Pittsburgh, as the most widely copied of architectural forms in late-nineteenth-century America.

Two years after the dedication of the church, Richardson designed a red-brick, sandstone-trimmed parsonage for Phillips Brooks just a block away. The center of its two-and-half-story, double-gabled western facade frames an asymmetrical low-sprung arch creating a deeply recessed entrance porch. Decorative panels between the windows of the second story contain cut brick floral patterns, and a projecting bay on the south culminates in a molded brick chimney. The design of Brooks's home occupied a great deal of office attention, and many studies survive for the whole and its details, especially of the southern chimney. The parsonage survives significantly remodeled.

Richardson's work for Phillips Brooks at the parsonage was deft, but his work at Trinity Church was pivotal. It established him as an architect of note here and abroad, and it gave him the excuse to move from New York to Massachusetts, from Staten Island to Brookline. That relocation must always have seemed inevitable. The only question would have been when. By the spring of 1874 the time was ripe; he was in Brookline by June. With his return to New England the architect began the most productive dozen years of his life.

7 ❖ BROOKLINE 1874–82

THE ENGINEER ERNEST BOWDITCH, A SUBCONTRACTOR IN CHARGE OF driving the pilings under Trinity Church, thought Richardson's backlog of New England friends made it easy for him to attain social position when he moved back to the Boston area, a position that might have taken others years to reach. He was right, for old school ties continued to serve the architect well. Edward "Ned" Hooper, Richardson's classmate at college, became treasurer of the Harvard Corporation in 1876 and commissioned both Sever and Austin Halls from the architect. Scion of a wealthy and socially prominent family, Hooper belonged to a circle of artists, scholars, connoisseurs, and collectors that included the members of his extended family as well as Richardson, John La Farge, and Augustus Saint-Gaudens. The first American to recognize the genius of English poet and illustrator William Blake, he served as trustee of the Museum of Fine Arts and collected the works of J. M. W. Turner and Winslow Homer. Like his sisters, Ellen Gurney and Marian "Clover" Adams, for both of whom Richardson was to design houses, Hooper eventually ended his own life.

In 1864 young Hooper had bought the old Samuel Gardner Perkins place on Cottage Street in Brookline. In the spring of 1874 he rented it to H. H. Richardson and his family. The house sat on a two-acre site at the top of the rise from Jamaica Pond to Warren Street. A rambling two-story frame structure fronted by slender colossal piers upholding a low, overhanging hip roof, it dated from early in the century. It was one of a number of similar Federal style farmhouses in the area that are called locally "Jamaican planter's houses." The building must have reminded the architect somewhat of the great houses of the river road he had known in his youth in Louisiana. We know his assistants Charles Coolidge and Welles Bosworth thought it did. In the Perkins house Richardson lived and worked surrounded by his sustaining brood of children and helpers for the rest of his life.

There was more to Richardson's move to Brookline than the friendship of Hooper or the availability of the Perkins house. Brookline was a "wealthy and beautiful suburban town," according to a Massachusetts gazetteer published the year Richardson arrived, and two years after his death another source called it "the wealthiest in the United States." The suburb was independent, having fought off the acquisitive grasp of Boston to remain free of urban politics. And it

was self-assured—the location of the first country club in the nation, an exclusive social enclave founded in 1882 that has never felt the need to call itself anything but the Country Club. Richardson of course became a member.

The rolling parkland west of Jamaica Pond had long attracted attention as an agreeable homesite for successful men. The author and landscape architect Andrew Jackson Downing wrote in 1840 that the area formed a "kind of landscape garden," that nowhere else in the country existed anything "so inexpressibly charming as the lanes which lead from one cottage, or villa, to another." He thought it possessed an "Acadian air of rural freedom and enjoyment." Richardson's first biographer, Mariana Van Rensselaer, who knew the area well, later described the district as "naturally picturesque—richly wooded, everywhere rolling, in some parts really hilly, and often boldly broken by huge ledges of rock." One draftsman remembered moss-covered rocks along the road, a brook tumbling over its bed, long lines of New England stone fences with rich meadows beyond, and now and then an old colonial farmhouse "gray with time"—a suggestive landscape for the home and office of a collaborator of Frederick Law Olmsted who would develop an architecture of geological analogy, an architecture in which buildings became one with their natural surroundings.

Van Rensselaer thought all the homes in the area had "personality," but she especially singled out that of Charles Sprague Sargent. The son of a wealthy merchant and three years Richardson's junior, Sargent had joined the Union army after graduation from Harvard, in 1862. A dendrologist, trained in the taxonomy of trees and woody plants, he had by 1873 become the first director of Harvard's Arnold Arboretum. Sargent was also one of the directors of the Boston & Albany Railroad, and from that position he would send work Richardson's way. So close to Richardson did he become that after the architect's death he joined Olmsted in commissioning the Van Rensselaer biography. A number of other prominent men lived within walking distance of Sargent's 150-acre estate, called Holm Lea, across Cottage Street from the Perkins house. The large comfortable homes of these civic and social leaders dotted the landscape.

Brookline represented just the right domestic situation for a young and coming architect with professional and social ambitions for himself and his family. As Richardson's colleague Peter B. Wight wrote at the time of his death, the architect chose to live in Brookline, "where he was surrounded by the friends of his wife and the refined and cultured society whose association and sympathy he craved." Richardson was a climber who aspired to social equality with his neighbors; Brookline was the right base camp. It should be said, however, that in trying to keep up with the Sargents and other wealthy suburbanites, in trying to live as well as his friends and clients, Richardson spent everything he earned and then some. This was an attitude he seems to have passed on to Stanford White, with even more unfortunate results, for both men were to die deeply in debt.

Life in Brookline was a somewhat rough-and-tumble collection of parents, children, and draftsmen, the family reaching its full strength in 1876 with the birth of Frederick Leopold William Richardson. As the architect's oldest child, Julia Richardson Shepley, later recalled, the six children all thought they shared in their father's work. When ideas came to him at family suppers they would be sent running for drawing materials, "and as we hung over him he would consult us as to doors and windows." No wonder he spawned generations of architects. Jula, as she was known, accompanied her father in the goddard buggy when he drove out with his pair of fine horses to inspect his local buildings. She also remembered the excitement of riding with him in winter smothered in furs in his two-seated, boat-shaped sleigh. He would toss coins to children as they passed and they would call him Santa Claus. "He always had some of us children with him," she wrote, "and we revelled in it, he was so gay and full of fun."

Richardson worked at home surrounded by his wife and children, yet no descendant can remember ever seeing a photograph of him with any members of his family. Some show him in the office with a few draftsmen, but no informal snapshots exist with his wife, Julia, or the offspring. This might seem odd in our camera-ridden era, but Richardson in fact died before the concept and the capability of taking snapshots became general. The camera still served a formal role.

During these years Richardson began to lose the slenderness of his youth and assume the enlarged proportions of his later life. A studio portrait taken in

H. H. Richardson in Brookline, Massachusetts, 1879. By the late 1870s, the slender student had begun to take on the hefty proportions of the mature architect.

1879 shows him alone, his girth greatly expanded and his barrel shape silhouetted against a shakily painted landscape. His dark hair and beard frame deep intense eyes, but his face begins to look puffy. There is something disjointed about this formal photograph. His accessories are fine—he holds gloves and walking stick in his left hand and a straw planter's hat in the other—but his huge double-breasted suit coat appears to have been freshly plucked from some packing case. His increased bulk no doubt required new clothes, but it is surprising that a man who told his daughter that his "dress suit was his fortune" would permit himself to be immortalized in such wrinkled attire.

Richardson's clothing now had to accommodate an increasingly enlarged body produced by a combination of illness and indulgence. The healthy regime of exercise and cold baths he had followed on Staten Island during his idle days in the previous decade gave way to the demands of a busy professional life as well as the delights of society. In the midst of the rich social milieu available to him in the Boston area, Richardson returned to the generous hosting of his Harvard days. He joined all the right organizations, including the famous Saturday Club, founded by the likes of Emerson, Longfellow, and Holmes. Occasionally he entertained another group of gentlemen dedicated to the gustatory arts, the Winter's Night Club, at home in the low-ceiling dining room, the walls of which he had painted blood red. According to his daughter a series of round black oak tops for the dining table could expand it from the usual twelve to the "Club table" that seated twenty-four. "It was magnificent," she added. On these "lavish" occasions, according to Charles Coolidge, the host might serve wines from old cellars in New Orleans, oysters from Baltimore, and terrapin—which Mark Twain had declared lent a "royal flavor" to any feast—direct from M. F. Augustin's Walnut Street restaurant in Philadelphia, "with a chef in attendance all the way."

Richardson's Rabelaisian intake did not end with such festive occasions, however. The sculptor Augustus Saint-Gaudens seems a reliable guide to other times with the architect in a familial setting, at table with his wife and "round-faced, expectant children." Before dinner he would say to his guest, "S-S-Saint-Gaudens, ordinarily I lead a life of a-abstinence, but to-night I am going to break my rule to celebrate your visit, you come so rarely." He would then call for a magnum of champagne, which had to be finished by the two men. Since Saint-Gaudens drank little, Richardson consumed most of the two-quart bottle, accompanied, of course, by enormous amounts of cheese. Both wine and cheese were proscribed by his doctor, who was following the recommendations of the latest medical publications on kidney diseases, the symptoms of which the architect had begun to show. "The proceeding doubtless occurred every night," Saint-Gaudens remarked, "as he always arranged to bring home a guest."

Such high living was bound to have repercussions, and Richardson's health problems began to mount. His hernia continued to cause trouble. In a letter to

H. H. Richardson in the east parlor of the Perkins house in Brookline, c. 1880. Before Richardson built his own library, he worked in one of the rooms in his rented house surrounded by his collection of decorative objects, including the armchair in the foreground, one of a type he designed for the Winn Memorial Library in 1878.

Olmsted of August 1876, Richardson reported that, after the finding of a medical examination that his "parts [were] very much engorged," he had been ordered to bed for a week. A series of doctors puzzled over his case, he wrote, and raised the idea of an operation, but he would resist anything that endangered his life "on account of my wife & babies." Despite the medical advances of the century, Richardson seems to have considered surgery a great risk. Three years later, in November 1879, Olmsted wrote to Prof. Charles Eliot Norton of Harvard that the architect was on his back for three months because of his hernia, "in a most irksome and depressing and I should think somewhat hazardous position." But, he continues, "I found him very lively in mind with his draughtsmen about him, directing a great deal of interesting work."

Olmsted probably visited the architect in the second-floor room he added to the west side of the Perkins house. The chamber is reached by a stairway defined by spindle and latticework screens and lighted through windows divided into small panes of amber glass. Light floods into the squarish space from double windows on opposite walls, and broad window seats permit the occupants of the room to survey anyone approaching the house from the entrance gates. Since he was frequently flat on his back, Richardson hung rings from the perforated wooden ceiling above his bed so that by grasping them he might more easily shift his great weight. Above the matchboard wainscot he lined the walls with cork, "very soft and pleasing in appearance and texture," according to client John J. Glessner, on which he could pin up "fresh sketches" and photographs of work under consideration or in construction. There family, draftsmen, and clients alike would join him for discussion.

In New York the architect's life had been divided between his family on Staten Island and his work in Manhattan. The commuting life typified the capitalist-industrial era, which created the separation between the feminine domestic

C. Howard Walker, "Fire-place. Mr. Richardson's Study, Brookline," Massachusetts, ca. 1887. The architect's most personal room, in which he kept his collection of objects of Arts and Crafts virtù. (Collection of H. and S. Myers, Philadelphia)

establishment on the outskirts of the city and the masculine commercial enterprise downtown. In wooded Brookline the Perkins house became both home and workplace. The Cottage Street site supported a cottage industry that harkened back to a time when there had been no artificial separation between life and labor, between home and work. Such an ambience well suited Richardson's professional aims, and his aesthetic ones as well, for he wanted to rework the traditional architectures of the past, especially the Romanesque of France and Spain, and apply them to the society of the present, rather than incorporate the innovations of nineteenth-century industry.

At first the office remained in New York while Richardson worked out of the east parlor of the Perkins house, and Stanford White ran back and forth between the two. White doted on the children, especially Jula, whom he took skating in winter and fishing or bathing in summer. After 1878, with the office now moved to Brookline, Richardson began to add a series of drafting rooms to Ned Hooper's house. He directed the erection of a pair of wooden, one-story, flat-roofed sheds— the Coops, as they came to be called—with separate drafting alcoves and common office and exhibition space. These meandered off the east parlor and eventually culminated in a fireproof masonry structure housing Richardson's private study and library.

Richardson lavished attention on the furnishings of the library, his most intimate space and an extension of his own rich and expansive personality. It replaced the east parlor as the center of his world, and there he gathered around him the souvenirs of his life, work, and travels. A room some twenty-five by thirty feet, the library seemed to his awed assistants a "dreamland beyond" the workaday drafting Coops. The room held a cavernous fireplace in which "cordwood crackled gleefully." The interior was as deeply colored as Trinity Church: blue carpets, deep maroon walls, a solid gold ceiling with cherry beams, all overplayed by the rosy glow diffused from the skylight over a "bewildering mass of riches." To the draftsmen the room was a "magic source of inspiration," and, although it was intended as the architect's private retreat, generous as always, he permitted them to use it as well. There they found stashed away a collection of "Contes Drolatiques," or French comical tales, which one of them thought best showed the "broad sympathies and deep humanity of the master as nothing else could."

The room exhibited tiles, curtains, Oriental rugs, "stupendous volumes in sumptuous bindings," bric-a-brac, casts and vases, Oriental lamps, divans, drawings, and photographs. The bric-a-brac reflected the cosmopolitan dimensions of Richardson's interests. A probate inventory of the room taken just after his death lists works of the English and American Arts and Crafts Movement such as De Morgan vases, Rookwood (or Cincinnati) pottery, William Morris textiles, and a Morris hanging lamp. It included Persian vases, rugs, and lamps, Indian knives and an Indian fiddle, vases from Venice, Bombay, and Japan, a menorah, a Japanese cabinet, a Chinese bronze bowl, a Spanish trunk, an Italian dagger, and East Indian battle-ax and swords. Together with the books, drawings, and casts, the contents of the room formed an eclectic, Gilded Age treasure trove. The library had many uses, as we shall see, not least among them to awe the impressionable client or put off an expectant creditor.

After the success of Trinity Church, work might have poured into the Coops had it not been for the depression of the mid-seventies, which slowed new construction. Still, there was always work to do. "And what work!" as the architect would exclaim. The New York State Capitol, in Albany, presented the largest and most complex task. Construction of the new statehouse had began just after the Civil War, from designs in the Renaissance Revival style by architect Thomas Fuller. By 1874, however, the budget had been spent and the exterior walls had barely risen above the second story. A commission chaired by Lieut. Gov. William Dorsheimer, Richardson's client and friend, appointed an advisory committee of three to make a critical review of the work, a committee composed of Olmsted, Richardson, and New York architect Leopold Eidlitz. The report of the committee not only addressed problems of construction but, not surprisingly, suggested a revised design in the Romanesque style. Architects across the country protested the change in style and rightly questioned the propriety of the new architects criticizing the work of the old. To no avail. The commission dismissed

Senate Chamber, New York State Capitol, Albany, 1876–81. With the interior of Trinity Church, the Senate Chamber ranks among the most opulent and serene masterpieces of late-nineteenth-century American architecture.

Senate foyer, New York State Capitol, Albany, 1876–81. Space, light, Romanesque architectural forms, and custom-designed furniture combine here to create an aura of political power.

OPPOSITE: *Detail of fireplace and clock, New York State Court of Appeals, Albany, 1876–81. Richardson's designs for the woodwork and furniture of this courtroom exemplify his concern for the totality of the design process and his anticipation of the ideals of the Arts and Crafts Movement.*

Fuller and in 1876 hired Olmsted, Richardson, and Eidlitz to finish the building.

Further political and architectural intrigues slowed the work considerably. The legislature entered the debate about style in 1877, when it insisted that the building be finished in Fuller's Italian Renaissance forms. Francophile Richardson would have none of that. He suggested to Olmsted that he believed "entre-nous that the building can be well finished in Francis Ier or Louis XIV which come under the head of Renaissance." In the end the commission approved a revised version of the replacement design, one that better harmonized with what had already been built, and work began.

The architects divided design responsibility, with Eidlitz taking charge of the Assembly side of the Capitol and Richardson the Senate. Stanford White still assisted the architect, who entrusted him with both legwork and design work, the latter, of course, under the master's supervision. Richardson aimed for "simplicity and quietness" in the Senate chamber, he told Olmsted in May 1876, correcting anything in White's splendid drawings that worked against that effect and sending them off to New York with his assistant. As he so often did when writing even business letters to his friend, Richardson complained about his health. "I am sick," he wrote, and "in considerable pain." For the rest of his life this combination of work and sickness became a refrain, the work almost seeming to profit from his indispositions, to gain what Shakespeare called the "benefit of ill."

The definitive design of the chamber was not established this early, however. Instead, revision followed revision. In a letter written two years later, White told Saint-Gaudens, whom he was soon to join in Paris, that he had just paid his last visit "to the abode of the Great Mogul . . . and there tackled the Albany Senate Chamber, and between us I think we have cooked up something pretty decent." After tantalizing the sculptor with thoughts of acres of carved marble panels, he summarized the design: "The whole room is to be a piece of color." That is, Richardson intended it to be the secular equivalent of the interior of Boston's Trinity Church, which had been dedicated the previous year. The room as lately restored remains, with Trinity, one of the richest and yet calmest of American Victorian spaces. When finished, the New York Senate chamber became, according to a contemporary observer, "the most beautiful room in America," but that distinction was in fact a toss-up between sacral Boston and secular Albany.

Richardson designed other parts of the Capitol in addition to the Senate

Ornamental detail, New York State Court of Appeals, Albany, 1876–81. For Richardson, the proof of his work was in its materialization, for no drawing could suggest the amplitude of carving such as this.

Detail of chair and desk, New York State Court of Appeals, Albany, 1876–81. Richardson's furniture exhibited the love of natural materials and tactile surfaces that marked the Arts and Crafts Movement.

chamber: the governor's office, the western staircase, the New York State Library, and the Court of Appeals. Others altered and executed some of his ideas. The Senate chamber was never completed in his lifetime, but the Court of Appeals was, and furnished from his designs. The architect's office supplied drawings for furniture and other decorative arts when the budget permitted. How much of this actually came from his hand is uncertain, although he surely approved the designs of such assistants as Francis Bacon and the execution of furniture makers such as A. H. Davenport. The paneled woodwork, seating, and especially the tall case clock created for the courtroom show Richardson by the early 1880s designing total interior environments on the model of the English Arts and Crafts Movement, inspired by William Morris.

The nineteenth-century design community harbored a range of attitudes toward change. Some embraced the transformations in society as well as production wrought by the Industrial Revolution, some did not, and others found themselves drawn to some forms of machine production while repudiating other forms. Some architects and designers embraced the new industrial materials, not just for structural assistance or visible effect but for the economy industrial techniques might introduce into production. William Morris and his followers in the Arts and Crafts Movement sought to restore medieval handicraft production, and they naturally tried to avoid the machine in their efforts to base their work on medieval precedent. In his furniture as in his buildings, Richardson followed suit as he sought to create a preindustrial ambience.

Richardson built two buildings for his alma mater after Ned Hooper became treasurer of the Harvard Corporation. The differences between Sever and Austin

West front of Sever Hall, Harvard University, Cambridge, Massachusetts, 1878–80. Sever exemplifies Richardson's use of traditional forms realized in preindustrial materials such as plain, carved, and molded brickwork.

Halls, designed within two years of each other, spring from their different sites and uses but, more important, from the fact that Sever was erected for a fixed amount left by a deceased donor while Austin's benefactor was alive and vulnerable to the pleadings of Hooper and Richardson for more and more money.

In early 1877 the widow of alumnus James Warren Sever left at her death $100,000 for the erection of a building in memory of her husband. In April 1878, the college empowered an old-boy committee consisting of Hooper and one of Henry Adams's brothers, John Quincy Adams, to ask Richardson for a design. The architect's commission had by now been established as 5 percent of total cost, so he received $5,000 for his design and working drawings, but he also received an additional $1,200 for supervision. Hooper himself paid some incidental architectural fees. Norcross erected the building in 1879.

A year or so later Edward Austin, a Beacon Hill merchant who had not attended Harvard, offered the college another $100,000 for a law school building, to be erected to the memory of his brother Samuel. A long period of negotiations involving President Charles Eliot, Dean Christopher Langdell, Richardson, Norcross, the donor, and Hooper as arbiter resulted in a final gift of more than $140,000. Richardson's commission of 7 percent included supervision: he received $9,529.58 for his work when Austin was finished by Norcross, in 1884.

Brick Sever and stone Austin represent two rather different strands in Richardson's work. Sever takes some of its cues from the Federal style buildings across Harvard Yard but is otherwise free of historical cant. The exterior superbly exemplifies his "quiet" architecture and stands as a textbook illustration of the imaginative use of restricted materials, including nothing more than roof tiles and plain, molded, and carved brickwork. It is characteristic of Richardson's craft-oriented, conservative technological bent that the ornament, here as on Trinity parsonage, is carved brick rather than cast terra-cotta, an industrial product recently reintroduced into architecture. Sever also features what became another signature detail of his work, the low-sprung Syrian arch facing the yard.

Austin Hall welds the parti of Richardson's contemporary library designs, as we shall see, to Romanesque forms he visited about this time on a trip to the south of France. The exterior incorporates Richardsonian characteristics such as rough-faced random ashlar stonework set in red mortar, horizontal layering, and a symmetrical front compromised by the asymmetrical stair tower, but these seem almost formulaic, as if the architect were copying himself rather than giving the work the benefit of fresh thought. Richardson's conservative design here, unlike his best work, has a lifeless effect. Austin proves that a larger budget does not necessarily a better building make.

Richardson's practice extended beyond government and educational buildings to encompass many of the structures required by the society of his day. During the 1870s and 1880s American society began to crystallize into the polar pattern it maintains to the present: a series of urban matrices formed of dense commercial cores surrounded by sprawling domestic suburbs, the two connected first by commuter railroads and then by automobile freeways. This evolving social pattern during Richardson's working life generated two distinctly American building types: the downtown office building, which would sprout into the skyscraper after his death, and the detached single-family house nestled into the wooded outskirts. It would also call forth other building types, such as suburban cultural centers, public libraries, and commuter railway depots. Under the guidance of his mentor Olmsted, Richardson developed differential solutions to the needs of all these new building programs.

The downtown commercial work that culminated in Richardson's memorable Marshall Field Wholesale Store in Chicago in 1885 began ten years earlier

with a building he designed for his father-in-law's heirs. Although basic income property, the five-story Hayden Building in central Boston is a focal work in Richardson's career. Its exterior stonework shows that Richardson had looked at the earlier works of the Boston Granite style. Especially the "building-block" quality of the exterior design at the upper floor points to that precedent, while the two-story arcade of the third and fourth floors anticipates the articulation of the Field Store.

The facade of the R. and F. Cheney block at Hartford, begun by Norcross in 1875, intervened between the Hayden and Field buildings. The Cheney brothers manufactured silk products in a nearby planned industrial community and needed an outlet in the city. The plan of their Hartford building—now changed—had a central court surrounded by commercial spaces. The surviving Main Street facade exhibits a disciplined exuberance. Three horizontal zones marked by ornamental belt courses open through lively arcades, whose scale diminishes toward the cornice. The end bays rise above the others, that on the right higher than that on the left. When Richardson told a reporter in Chicago in 1885 that he had long studied commercial facades, he referred especially to the Hayden and Cheney buildings.

A good number of upper-middle-class people still lived in cities in this era, and Richardson designed several urban dwellings for this class. The parsonage for Phillips Brooks was followed by a residence on K Street at Sixteenth in Washington, D.C., for Nicholas Longworth Anderson. A member of a wealthy Cincinnati clan, Anderson had been a Harvard classmate of the architect. He

LEFT: *Facade, Cheney Brothers Building, Hartford, Connecticut, 1875–76. An urban outlet for the silk manufacturers of nearby South Manchester, this was one of a number of commercial works Richardson designed in the last decade of his life.*

RIGHT: *Exterior detail of the Cheney Brothers Building, Hartford, Connecticut, 1875–76. The materials and forms of Richardson's mature buildings owed much to his earlier interest in the granite works of his predecessors in Boston.*

enlisted as a private in an Ohio regiment during the Civil War and emerged a brevet major general. In 1881 he budgeted $33,000 for the house; its final cost pushed $100,000. Anderson proved to be putty in the architect's hands. Clover Adams, who with her husband was to order a Washington house from Richardson within a few years, cattily remarked that clients like Anderson and Francis Lee Higginson, just then building a Richardson house in the Back Bay section of Boston, "don't know their own minds, though the proportions are not excessive in either case." As a result they found themselves irritatingly incapable of resisting the blandishments of the architect, "who sets many temptations before them as it's his business" to do. Indeed, the descriptions of the architect given by both the general and his wife do less than flatter the man.

Clover Adams was here being typically sarcastic, but there is fact in what she wrote. After he returned from his trip abroad in the summer of 1882, Richardson visited the Anderson house. "His pleasure . . . is worth seeing," the general's wife wrote to their son, "and he proposed so many more nice (and expensive) additions that it made my head swim and drove your father into a melancholy from which he has not recovered yet. . . . the interior is tempting for decoration and Mr. Richardson will not let us off so easily." Although the house has been demolished, photographs show its rather austere brick-box exterior enriched with a round tower, a polygonal bay, a high roof, and carved brick ornament that hid its richly paneled interior. Its massive, almost martial simplicity drew fire from the neighbors, and apparently from Henry Adams himself, but the general was not swayed by public opinion. "It requires a severe and well-educated taste to see in its grand lines and simple beauty all that we claim for it," he wrote. "I am delighted with it. . . . But, oh, how big it looks!" And how much it cost!

Out from the urban centers, in the Boston suburbs and along the Massachusetts seashore, Richardson's domestic commissions called for a natural site and an informal expression. There, in the Bryant house in Cohasset, the Browne house in Marion, and the Stoughton house in Cambridge, Richardson began to use what has come to be called the Shingle style. These houses grew from his earlier work at Newport, with living halls the foci of asymmetrical plans and relaxed rambling exteriors covered ground line to roof ridge with wooden shingles. They are Victorian elaborations on the simple wooden houses of the colonial period.

The commission for the Stoughton house came into the office in 1882, just as Richardson was preparing to leave for a summer trip to England and the Continent. Norcross built it for Mary Fisk Stoughton, the widowed mother of the philosopher John Fiske, an 1863 graduate of Harvard who later joined the faculty in history. A broad hall with fireplace and entrance beneath the staircase centered an L-shaped plan characteristic of the architect's mature domestic work. The various units of the exterior are simple geometric forms surrounding the inner volumes. Tight shingled surfaces flow together; the horizontal line prevails.

Main front of the Mary Fisk Stoughton house, Cambridge, Massachusetts, 1882–83. The irregular forms, tight surfaces, generous openings, and prevailing horizontal lines are all characteristic of the architect's mature Shingle style houses.

Exterior detail of the Mary Fisk Stoughton house, Cambridge, Massachusetts, 1882–83. The look of Richardson's domestic architecture varied from city to suburb, from urbane red-brick or ashlar masonry houses near urban centers to irregular granite-boulder or wood-shingle forms appropriate to suburb and seashore.

The exterior of Richardson's Stoughton house has been justly celebrated, but the interior has always disappointed. The cause for this disjunction may be assigned to a rupture between architect and client, expressed in a letter from the architect dated August 1883. Richardson had returned from a trip to find a series of letters from his client containing numerous complaints. It seemed useless to him to consider them, as some seemed unreasonable and others untrue. "Since you insist on continuing to consider yourself imposed upon," he wrote, "I think it best for all concerned that I should withdraw from any further charge of the erection of your house." He would consider it a favor if she would consult someone else about the finishing of the interior, "some architect in whom you have more confidence." He was sorry about this, he insisted, but he felt that Mary Stoughton had misunderstood him from the beginning. Richardson said he had been especially interested in the house because it was to be built on a very visible site in Cambridge near the college. And finally, because of his regard for her son, he had persuaded Norcross to undertake the construction on the basis of a dangerously low bid.

Such poor public relations were rare in Richardson's career. His hurt at having been shabbily treated by an ungrateful client radiates, unstated but implied, from this letter. That he was a man's man and she a woman who knew her own mind may have contributed significantly to the lack of understanding between the two of them.

In the 1870s and early 1880s, Richardson began working on two other suburban building types that have helped to establish his lasting reputation: the small-town public library and the commuter railroad depot. He also began a series of commissions for the Ames family in North Easton, Massachusetts, in Boston, and elsewhere that would make them collectively his most important patrons.

Richardson erected the series of small suburban libraries in a ring around Boston. They represent a combination of the flowering of popular education in the post–Civil War era and a new spirit of public philanthropy. Often cultural centers containing collections of art and natural history, and lecture rooms as well as book depositories, these institutions brought learning to a wide audience at the same time that they memorialized men who had helped build small-town America. They did not, however, please the members of the newly formed American Library Association, who objected to spending money on what they considered frills rather than necessities, on civic landmarks rather than storage facilities. The librarians fought against the concept of the traditional gentleman's library

that formed the core of Richardson's buildings, with their richly paneled book rooms surrounded with tiered alcoves, their comfortable reading rooms warmed by richly wrought fireplaces. The librarians' association wanted the readers separated from books, which would be efficiently stored in hidden metallic book stacks of a kind that became standard after their first use, at Harvard's library in the mid-seventies.

Richardson designed his first libraries for Woburn, North Easton, and Quincy, Massachusetts, between 1876 and 1882. He won the commission for the Winn Memorial, in Woburn, in competition with several other local firms; that for the Crane Memorial, in Quincy, came directly to him, perhaps at the recommendation of the chairman of the building committee, Charles Francis Adams Jr., another of Henry's brothers. These buildings are filled with his signature details: an articulation of the plan into its various components; in the interior, book-lined alcoves superbly executed by Norcross and memorials to the donors carved by Saint-Gaudens; on the exterior, an asymmetrical composition of rock-faced random ashlar set in red mortar, various forms reflecting the internal organization, clearly marked entrances, and handsomely carved, Romanesque-inspired details.

The library in North Easton, whose simpler design Richardson preferred to Woburn's, marked the beginning of the architect's work for the Ames family. The first Oliver Ames moved to North Easton in 1803 to establish a shovel factory powered by the abundant waterfall in the area. Ames sold his shovels nationwide: in fact, Richardson's family's firm, the Priestley and Bein Hardware Company in New Orleans, carried them during his youth. Oliver's sons, Oaks and Oliver II, saw the company prosper through the Civil War and the building of the transcontinental railroad. Shovel making became a stepping-stone to financing the Union

Pacific Railroad and the acquisition, in the next generation, of large real estate holdings. At his death, Oliver II left $50,000 for a library, a gesture that began what one historian has called the "aesthetic transformation" of the industrial village, for which Richardson ultimately designed more than five buildings, including the prominently placed Ames Memorial Hall, adjacent to the library.

Oliver II's bequest was executed by his children, Frederick Lothrop and Helen Angier Ames. F.L., three years older than the architect, graduated from Harvard in Charles Gambrill's class and eventually became one of Richardson's most important clients. They also became close friends, a fact that points to the strength of Harvard cement in bonding together unlikely types. Sources describe F. L. Ames as a "cold, forceful, unostentatious" man and a "power in industrial circles." He was eventually to become a director or official of some sixty railroads, an officer of banks and trust companies, one of the largest owners of Boston real estate, and a fellow of Harvard College.

The Ames library project entered the office about the time of the architect's thirty-ninth birthday, in September 1877; the building was under construction during the next year. Richardson's plan lined up alcoved book room, entrance hall, and reading room, and fronted them with an asymmetrically placed cross gable with low-arched entrance beneath a powerful Romanesque arcade at the level of the librarian's apartment. Vertical circulation is clearly marked on the exterior by the tower rising between the opposed building masses; in fact, all the elements of the plan are legible from the outside. A rooster and an owl carved on the imposts of the entrance to the library symbolically admonish visitors to "wake up" and "get wise."

The chief feature of the reading room is a fireplace richly decorated with floral motifs and a memorial portrait of Oliver II, all finely detailed by Saint-Gaudens. The book room to the left is a two-story alcoved space crowned by a barrel vault, the entire interior executed in carved and turned butternut wood. On the exterior of this wing Richardson introduced another signature: three superimposed horizontal zones—ashlar base, window frieze, and tiled roof. This layered look emphasizes the sense of ground-hugging repose that Richardson sought in much of his mature work, and it was to inspire the horizontal Prairie style architecture of Frank Lloyd Wright.

Outlying towns and villages like North Easton worked only because they were connected by an umbilical railroad to the commercial center. The Ames family created a commuter spur linking its homes and factory to roads leading out from Boston, and in 1881 F. L. Ames commissioned from Richardson a depot to be erected near the entrance to his estate. Richardson began designing such commuter stations in 1881, when the Boston & Albany Railroad commissioned his first, for Auburndale Center in Newton, Massachusetts. Old friends ran the line—

Pres. Chester Chapin and Vice Pres. James Rumrill—and Richardson's Brookline neighbor Charles Sprague Sargent sat on the board of directors. They sent a series of depots his way during the last years of his life, most of them designed either for the B&A's commuter loop or for its main line, running westward out of the city.

The design of F. L. Ames's depot at North Easton followed the lead Richardson established in his work for the B&A. At the functional level the task called for a sheltered point of transition between two modes of transportation, between the private carriages that brought customers to the track and the trains that ran between city and suburb. At the expressive level these depots formed emblematic gateways heralding two institutions. On the one hand they reassuringly evoked the solid conservatism underpinning of the progressive system of railroad transportation, and on the other they framed the middle-class domestic values of the new suburban centers. Common features in all the depots are the imposing ashlar masonry walls beneath prominent roofs; a porte cochere, or covered carriageway, facing the suburb; separate waiting rooms flanking a central ticket office; and trackside sheds protecting the traveler from waiting room to train.

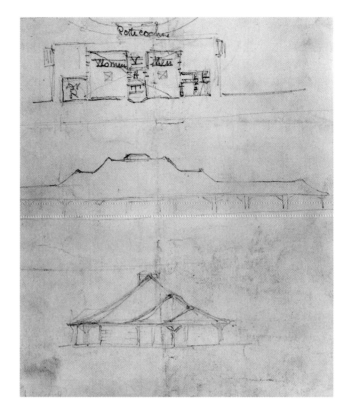

H. H. Richardson, preliminary sketch for the Old Colony Railroad Depot, North Easton, Massachusetts, 1881. Richardson's characteristic initial impulse envisions a ground-hugging, roof-sheltered way station for suburban commuters. (Printing and Graphic Arts, Houghton Library, Harvard University, Cambridge, Massachusetts)

Richardson's ideogram for the North Easton station sketched in these required spaces and sheltered them with an umbrellalike roof, horizontal, hipped, and flowing outward from a central chimney over the waiting areas below. He bore down heavily with his pencil when drawing the ridge line in order to emphasize the protective, ground-hugging qualities he sought in this as in other buildings. His second set of sketches firmed up and simplified the plan and indicated circulation paths from carriage around ticket office to train. They also introduced the five free-standing low arches that create the three-dimensional form and give the depot its dramatic spatial quality and its emblematic status as gateway.

The nineteenth century created a confrontation between industry and nature characterized by the cultural historian Leo Marx as "the machine in the garden." The machine in question was the train, and Richardson's North Easton depot acted as an intermediary between the railroad tracks leading away from the country and the view of the woods, meadows, and waterways of the Ames estate landscaped by Olmsted. As commuters emerged from the waiting room they caught sight of that landscape framed by the semicircular porte cochere arch. Although it served as gateway to the railroad, Richardson's ground-hugging, load-bearing masonry depot belonged more to nature than to industry.

Office of H. H. Richardson, Boylston Street Bridge, Back Bay Fens, Boston, Massachusetts, 1880. For Frederick Law Olmsted's Fens, Richardson created a geological analogy, a man-made structure that seems to merge with the landscape. (Printing and Graphic Arts, Houghton Library, Harvard University, Cambridge, Massachusetts)

If the depot interceded between machine and garden, the gate lodge F. L. Ames commissioned in 1880 for that landscape (the estate he called Langwater) seems to "nestle in nature," to quote Ralph Waldo Emerson in another context, and draw its meaning "from her roots and grains." The lodge grew from a collaboration between Richardson, Olmsted, Ames, and Norcross (with a few sculpted accents by Saint-Gaudens). It contains a potting shed to the left of the great archway and bachelor's quarters upstairs in the wing to the right. Beneath a horizontally flowing orange-tile roof, whose eaves gently curve in response to the polychromatic voussoirs of the central opening, the building seems like a cairn, or better, a glacial moraine. It is, to appropriate an apt phrase of Emily Dickinson, "a House that seemed/a Swelling of the Ground."

The thick walls of the Ames gate lodge are piles of local boulders, polished by the mechanics of the Ice Age, covered with lichen, and trimmed with East Longmeadow sandstone. Richardson worked with nature in buildings like this, enlarging upon ideas that originated in eighteenth-century England and were naturalized in America by his and Olmsted's predecessors, the architect Alexander Jackson Davis and the landscape designer Andrew Jackson Downing. We may also see in this design the impact of charismatic Louis Agassiz on Richardson during his undergraduate years, or the environmental concerns of Olmsted, or both, for here the architect achieved a geological analogy, a dramatic architectural celebration of the glacial landscape on which this building sits, or, better, from which it seems to emerge like the moraines and granite ledges so characteristic of New England. Richardson had traveled far from his student days in Paris, for he was now creating architecture not solely out of history but out of natural history as well, an American architecture for the American land. To visitors ap-

proaching this building there is no question that it belongs where it is; in fact, one cannot conceive of its ever not being there.

The collaboration of Olmsted and Richardson extended beyond North Easton in these years. Charles H. Dalton, one of the architect's clubby friends, chaired the Boston Park Commission, for which Olmsted laid out the Back Bay Fens and Richardson designed two bridges early in 1880. The railway span, now gone, was one of the rare metallic works of Richardson's career. The surviving Boylston Street Bridge is a superbly sculpted span of random ashlar masonry with a low segmental archway leaping between rounded abutments that seems to spring from nature itself. This is true of the completed work, and it is even more true of the structure as it appears in the panoramic sketch created in Richardson's office. The bridge demonstrates complete collaboration between architect and landscape architect, between man and nature, between architecture and geology. The same is true of the man-made mountain Richardson designed at this time in memory of Oakes and Oliver Ames out in Sherman, Wyoming, a monument conceived as a conventionalized outcropping and quarried from a real one. It was easy to mistake it for a natural object from a train running along the nearby Union Pacific tracks.

By the early 1880s Richardson's life and career had settled into the Brookline landscape and assumed the pattern they were to follow for the rest of his days—but with one notable exception. In the summer of 1882 he took a break, traveling to England and the Continent to visit the monuments of the past that had inspired his work and to recharge his faculties for the future.

8 ❖ EUROPE
1882

IN THE SUMMER OF 1875 RICHARDSON AND JULIA HAD JOINED OLM-
sted and his wife, Mary, on a vacation tour that Richardson insisted on calling a
"wedding trip," presumably because they visited Niagara Falls and because he and
his wife had had no honeymoon in 1867. They traveled a loop that took them to
Buffalo, Montreal, Quebec, and the White Mountains of New Hampshire. In
matters of scenery the architect deferred to the landscape architect, who set the
itinerary until they reached Canada. When they got to the falls, Olmsted wrote,
Richardson (as have so many before him and since) sat quietly "for hours in one
place contemplatively enjoying the beauty." At Quebec, on the other hand, the
architect took control as he studied the ancient French farmhouses of the prov-
ince. As his English contemporary William Morris did with medieval cottages,
Richardson admired the fact that, in these farmhouses, "so much more had been
done to please," and lamented the lack of character in recent work in the States.

By the summer of 1882 Richardson had been working without a prolonged
break since that trip in 1875. He had been thinking about a European holiday for
some time, and in June he embarked without Julia on what proved to be an anything but relaxing three-month journey to London, Paris, southern France,
northern Italy, and northern Spain. The Continental trek alone took nine weeks
and covered more than thirty-two hundred miles—as the crow flies—by boat,
train, and carriage. After a slow beginning in England, he traveled, as he said, at
a "lightning" pace, trying to cram in visits to as many sites in the hot southern
European landscape as his strength would permit. Even with present conveniences such a trip would be trying, even for a healthy person. Richardson was
not a healthy person, and one aspect of the trip was medical, although the result
was not salubrious. He returned more exhausted than when he departed, but full
of renewed admiration for his beloved Romanesque architecture.

As usual, even in motion Richardson surrounded himself with sturdy fellows. His shipboard party included Phillips Brooks of Trinity Church and his
brother-in-law, the Reverend James Franks of Salem, as well as the Reverend
William McVickar of Philadelphia (later Episcopal bishop of Rhode Island), John
Codman Ropes, a distinguished Boston lawyer, and Herbert Jacques, a twenty-
five-year-old graduate of M.I.T. who was a draftsman in his studio. Richardson,
Brooks, and McVickar visited Continental sites together, and they formed an

OPPOSITE: *Exterior detail of the
F. L. Ames Gate Lodge, North
Easton, Massachusetts, 1880–81.
In his most characteristic works
Richardson eschewed both the
Gothic style and the new iron
structural forms embraced by
so many of his contemporaries.*

outstanding group. The forty-three-year-old architect approached six feet in height, but he was a runt compared to his companions. "Physically majestic" Brooks towered to six feet four inches, and McVickar, who was "built on extraordinarily large proportions," overtopped him by an inch or more. They collectively weighed 912 pounds, according to the architect's own reckoning. Anecdotes of their progress through Europe were legion and, apocryphal or not, probably preserve something of the impression they made. At a lecture where they sat separately, each stood in sequence of ascending height to announce his nationality and refute the speaker's thesis that the Americans were a puny race. By the time bulky McVickar drew himself up to his full stature, the lecturer had been drowned in audience uproar. On another occasion some street urchins asked the trio if the dwarfs were on the way, thinking these were the giants in some circus freak show. A third story, told by the architect's daughter Julia Richardson Shepley, has them on the lido in Venice trying to rent bathing suits large enough to cover them. At intervals each in turn appeared at the kiosk to ask for a suit until the attendant collapsed in a spasm of disbelief.

The group sailed for Liverpool in the third week in June on the recently commissioned Cunarder *Servia*. It was state-of-the-art naval architecture: the first large steel-hulled ship in the Atlantic service and the first to be lit with incandescent electric lights. Its first-class complement outnumbered that of any other ship, and some of its staterooms were fitted with Broadwood's patent lavatories. It soon became the paradigm of the comfortable liner.

For an architect often touted by historians for a presumed interest in the products of industry, Richardson apparently paid little attention to these modern improvements. He said the ship was "superb," but he gave its conveniences no space in his letter home, one of a series sent during the trip in the huge, angular handwriting that so aptly reflected his larger-than-life persona. What impressed him most about the crossing was the food—not the quality but the quantity. "I have done nothing that I can note but *eat*," he wrote to Julia and the children. "It seems impossible to read & one only waits for a meal & when that is over longs for the next." He ate five meals a day, he wrote, and slept soundly. He seems surprised to report no bad effects from the voyage.

If he found the food to his liking, he complained about the crowded conditions. The ship housed 543 first-class passengers, the most ever to cross the Atlantic on one bottom. He shared a stateroom on the main deck with Jacques. In the evening Brooks and McVickar, "non-professional" but "such intelligent" traveling companions, came to study photographs of the sites they were to visit. During the day he and his companions sat on deck beneath awnings wishing a wind would come up to blow all the women and most of the men from the crowded lounge chairs. Still, the weather proved good most of the way and the company much to his liking. He discussed travel in Spain and the construction of libraries with one of the Philadelphia Biddles. John Ropes turned out to be "an invaluable man for a sea voyage with his active brain & easy tongue." He was a Civil War historian, and Richardson found his discussion of the conflict "amusing." He would not want to change anyone in the party, he wrote, although he would have added Charles Sprague Sargent, his Brookline neighbor, and F. L. Ames, his North Easton client.

Richardson stayed nearly two weeks in London, despite the cold rainy weather, shopping, visiting friends old and new, sightseeing, and consulting with the queen's physician. It did not take him long to revisit Poole's on Savile Row to be refitted for a new wardrobe. (His measurements on deposit there had become woefully obsolete.) He ordered a truss for his hernia. He visited Batsford's to shop for architectural books, went to the Royal Institute of British Architects to look over the library there, and called on James Russell Lowell, poet and U.S. minister to the Court of St. James. Lowell had admired Richardson's Trinity Church as well as his other work back in Boston and Cambridge (and had always liked the tower of the Brattle Street Church without knowing the name of the architect) and gave him letters of introduction to Spanish contacts. In one, much to the traveler's delight, Lowell called Richardson "our most original Architect." He dined well, at the Bristol, at Claridge's, and at the Criterion. And he engaged a body servant, Henry Hiscock, to accompany him on the Continent.

He soon contacted his old friend from the École des Beaux-Arts R. Phené Spiers, now a well-established London architect and somewhat radical educator. They dined and partied. Spiers took him to see Whistler's former residence, the White house in Chelsea, designed in 1878 by E. W. Godwin; Spiers's own Collier house on the Embankment; and then to Bedford Park, the community designed by Richard Norman Shaw in the previous decade. Shaw had been an architect of special interest to Richardson in the 1870s, when Richardson designed the Watts Sherman house at Newport, although by the time of this trip Shaw's influence had waned. Richardson inspected the heating and ventilating system of the House of Parliament; the knowledge gained he would put to good use in the public buildings at Pittsburgh. He also visited the Kensington house of another architect he had particularly admired, the late William Burges. According to Herbert Jacques, who of course accompanied Richardson on his visits, the architect expressed disappointment with the building, although Richardson himself, with more characteristic tolerance toward the work of his peers, merely wrote he was surprised by some things but pleased on the whole. When George Shepley visited London the following year, he looked for a book on Burges's work for Richardson.

Richardson apparently bought decorative arts for some of his clients on this European sojourn. In England he visited William De Morgan, the maker of "astonishing" tiles, Edward Burne-Jones, the artist and designer, and William Morris himself; windows by the latter two enhance the interior of Trinity Church.

Exterior, F. L. Ames Gate Lodge, North Easton, Massachusetts, 1880–81. Living quarters, gateway, and potting shed assume discrete fieldstone forms, but they are tied into a unit by the sandstone beltcourse, continuous windows, repetitive details, and orange-tile roof.

Morris advised him about the quality of a Persian carpet at Durlacher and Marks, a carpet that later belonged to F. L. Ames and is now in the Museum of Fine Arts, Boston. He inspected Morris and Company's works at Merton Abbey, and the famous designer and budding socialist himself received Richardson "very cordially" at his home, Kelmscott house, on the Thames in Hammersmith. Jacques thought Morris, who was just four years older than the architect, took great interest in Richardson, and indeed, except in politics presumably, they had much in common besides appearance (Morris, too, was bearded and broad). Morris pleased the architect with his straightforward manner. The English designer, like Richardson, looked backward, past the nineteenth century, for inspiration in a preindustrial golden age. But there were differences too. Morris theorized; Richardson did not. Morris's theory led him to a heartfelt socialism; Richardson left no signs of a considered political philosophy.

Morris's *Hopes and Fears for Art*, new when Richardson acquired it at the time of his visit to Hammersmith, joined the books in Richardson's ample library. He may have bought this little gathering of some of the designer's lectures merely as a souvenir of his visit, but in the talk "The Prospects of Architecture in Civilization," the architect of the F. L. Ames gate lodge would have found sympathetic ideas. Morris describes a medieval house as the ideal house, as "a work of art and a piece of nature." It would be well built of timber and stone, "skillfully planned and well proportioned," with a bit of carving about the arched doorway. The Englishman believed that architecture, defined as the "union of the arts," was one of the most important things man could produce. These were ideas to which Richardson had fully subscribed.

Mrs. Morris, Jane Burden, joined the "aesthetes" who gathered for tea during Richardson's visit. She appeared "Pre-Raphaelite to a degree," presenting herself "in crushed, cranberry color'd silk, Baby waist, full puffed sleeves & green necklace," Richardson wrote to Julia, but then stopped, promising to supply greater detail when he got home. "It was surprising," he remarked, but we, alas, will never know why. Richardson must have arranged to visit Kelmscott house again on his way home from the Continent, for in a letter written to his daughter May at the end of August, Morris mused about his return. "Apropos of fat," he wrote, "I wonder when Mr. Richardson will turn up."

Finally, a major reason for the London visit was medical. Richardson's Boston doctors must have already diagnosed some form of kidney ailment. Perhaps they had discovered the extended presence of albumin in his urine. This, plus dropsy (or swelling) and other symptoms, is named as a primary symptom in the study of Bright's disease published by the Canadian doctor Charles Purdy in the year of Richardson's death. Probably through the intervention of Sir James Paget, president of the International Congress of Medicine, Richardson consulted Sir William Gull, sixty-six-year-old authority on renal disorders and physician extraordinary to Queen Victoria. Sir William was associated with Guy's Hospital in London, where in the 1820s that "giant of medicine" Charles Bright had described the disorder thought to afflict the architect. Nephritis, then called Bright's disease, can be acute or chronic; in the nineteenth century it was a killer.

Richardson reported Sir William's diagnosis to Julia. On his initial examination he was "not sure" about Bright's disease. He found the architect's heart "remarkably sound" and not to be the cause of Richardson's problems. On further examination he said that the architect had, in his view, a more treatable form of the illness, one that proceeded—not surprisingly—from his digestion. He suffered from Bright's disease of the kidneys, which caused albuminuria and associated

Living-room fireplace, F. L. Ames Gate Lodge, North Easton, Massachusetts, 1880–81. An inglenook of dark-green paneled settles, aquamarine tiles, and signs of the zodiac carved into the massive fireplace lintel create a cozy corner of the "bachelor's hall" upstairs in the Gate Lodge.

LEFT: *Exterior, F. L. Ames Gate Lodge, North Easton, Massachusetts, 1880–81. Like the stone walls edging New England fields, the Gate Lodge grew by the piling of one glacially formed granite boulder upon another, the whole tied together with sandstone trim and topped by crisp roofs.*

RIGHT: *Exterior detail, F. L. Ames Gate Lodge, North Easton, Massachusetts, 1880–81. The contrast between the glacially formed granite boulders of the massive walls and the dressed parti-colored voussoirs of the archway over the road exemplifies Richardson's subtly differentiated handling of natural materials.*

symptoms of indigestion, abdominal swelling, or dropsy, and edema, but spared his heart. He said that Richardson's kidneys "were not altogether unfaithful servants" as they not only threw off quantities of albumin but at times performed properly, leaving the urine in its correct weight. Sir William "preached prudence & care & regularity of living." He prescribed a drink of claret, lemon juice, and warm water. We do not know whether Sir William intended this to act as a vasodilator to improve circulation, a diuretic to flush the kidneys, a beverage to satisfy the thirst sometimes associated with kidney disease, or all three. We do know that Richardson found it not very palatable and—though he did not admit it to Julia—seems to have thought even less appetizing a life of prudence and care.

"Bright's disease" was then used as a generic term for a variety of kidney ailments resulting from a variety of causes. We know neither the specific form nor the cause of Richardson's problem. Sir William scarcely had time for a proper diagnosis of the illness, although he again examined the architect when Richardson returned to London at the end of his Continental tour. Nor do we have enough information to permit us to be more specific about it. We can say, however, with Charles Purdy's volume in hand and knowing that the architect's urine contained high levels of albumin, that Richardson's diet left much to be desired. Purdy states emphatically that a person with such a condition should avoid albuminous food such as eggs and cheese, and he forbade the use of alcohol. We have any number of witnesses who attest to the architect's breaking these fundamental dietary restrictions. He would not give in to the disease.

London was a mere stopover on the architect's summer itinerary, however. By Bastille Day, Brooks, McVickar, Franks, Jacques, and Richardson had checked into the Hôtel de L'Empire, on the rue Daunou, in Paris. The city was ablaze, carriages forbidden in the crowded streets, and people danced all night beneath their rooms. As an *ancien élève* of the École des Beaux-Arts, Richardson felt quite

at home despite some changes, but he knew his Paris and left almost immediately for unknown territory to the south.

Two days later the travelers had visited St.-Germain-des-Prés and Chartres and arrived at Le Mans. In the next week they breezed through the Auvergne, studying and collecting photographs of characteristic medieval monuments. Richardson had now reached one of the foci of his trip: the mature Romanesque architecture of the twelfth century in one of its more interesting regional variations. That was his aim, but not everyone's. "Architecture must be the main interest," wrote Brooks, but "art, life, and scenery shall not be forgotten."

The Auvergne contains a ruggedly volcanic, stony landscape etched by deep ravines and dotted with high *puys*, or geological domes, some of them the spectacular sites for medieval structures. At Clermont-Ferrand, Richardson viewed the church of Notre-Dame-du-Port with great enthusiasm, according to Jacques.

Exterior, F. L. Ames Gate Lodge, North Easton, Massachusetts, 1880–81. Richardson seemed to have formed such geological architecture by scooping out a glacial moraine and roofing it for human habitation.

St. Nectaire-le-Haut. On his trip through the Auvergne in France in 1882, Richardson collected photographs of the Romanesque monuments that caught his interest. (Richardson Photographic Collection, Loeb Library, Harvard Graduate School of Design)

The structure typified the heavy, lithic, Auvergnat Romanesque and stood as the central work of a cluster of like monuments in the vicinity. The exterior reflects the vaulted interior arrangement of long, three-aisled nave, transepts with tall octagonal tower above the crossing, apse, and ambulatory with radiating chapels. Geometrical wall patterns composed of red, brown, gray, and black local granites enliven the external surfaces. It must have confirmed in Richardson's mind his design of the exterior of Trinity Church.

The party took a side trip to the hot springs of Royat, where they dined and had a pleasant evening. From Clermont they must have traveled down the valley and through the deep gorge of the Allier River. The scenery in the area is rough and hardy, like the medieval buildings that extend the earth into the realms of man and God. At Issoire the pilgrims paused to visit the twelfth-century church of St.-Paul. Richardson bought a photograph showing the pyramidal silhouette of the east end, with characteristic tall tower and chevet of radiating chapels so like the east view of Trinity. Another overnight detour took them to St.-Nectaire-le-Haut, where the architect raved over the small squat church perched on a spectacular site high in the clouds. The design of the south portal, with a round relieving arch set above a peaked lintel, is characteristic of the region, and one Richardson was to recall in the main doorway at the John J. Glessner house in Chicago. The town of Brioude followed. There the twelfth-century church dedicated to St. Julien uses polychromatic regional stonework in an almost Victorian display. Richardson gave no description, but its lithic simplicity, Gallic order, and colorful patterns must have appealed to him.

From Brioude the party reached Nîmes, where the architect did not fail to admire the remains of classical antiquity. He mentions the baths, the amphitheater, and the Maison Carrée. The weather now turned intensely hot and slowed down the members of the party. Phillips Brooks remarked on the "quiet old towns, and queer, quaint churches, and kind, dirty people" of the region. He also recognized that the Romanesque churches of the Auvergne gave "the key to a great deal that is in Trinity." He was right, although it is doubtful that Richardson had visited them during his student days. But they certainly influenced his unsuccessful entry in the later competition for the cathedral in Albany. The request for that design reached him on this trip. No one wants work to stalk him on vacation, and Richardson was briefly miffed by the intrusion, but in fact for him it was all the same, all life, all work, all architecture.

The next leg of the journey took them away from the Auvergne on a zigzag from the Allier to the Rhone and beyond, through Avignon and Arles to St.-Gilles and Marseilles. At the Romanesque church of St.-Trophime in Arles, Richardson delighted in the cloister, with its round and pointed arches on coupled columns. He thought the twelfth-century portal, with columns resting on lions and Christ in judgment overhead, by far the best they had seen. He did not mention but surely admired the heavy yet graceful tower that rises in three stages over the crossing. (At Arles, Richardson remarked, the women are noted for their beauty. He had an eye for comeliness wherever it occurred.) The ruins of the apse of nearby St.-Gilles-du-Gard, the Cluniac pilgrimage priory, impressed him more than anything, especially its triple-arched entrance facade, which he had greatly admired "for so many years." He had known it only from photographs, made it the source for his studies of the entrance porch at Trinity, and now "felt its influence so differently." He must have enjoyed also the ashlar cliffs of twelfth-century domestic architecture so abundant in the town. Indeed, Richardson remarked metaphorically, he had the sense of being so "mentally and sentimentally stuffed with pâté de-foie-gras" that he expected to have "artistic indigestion" the rest of his life. The weather remained very hot, and at Marseilles and elsewhere the party rested and shopped.

Italy followed. They went by boat from Marseilles to Genoa to Leghorn, then to Pisa, where the celebrated Campo, the architectural grouping of leaning tower, cathedral, and baptistery, now ranked as the finest thing he had seen. The travelers rested a week in Genoa, "saw every junk-shop in town and hosts of paintings," according to Jacques, then headed for Florence. There, "what with architecture, sculpture, and painting, and ice-cold lemonade," Jacques wrote, "Richardson's cup was full to the brim." The courtyard and stairway of the Bargello, the frescoes in Santa Croce, and the art museums all captured his attention. His study of the Florentine palaces of the early Renaissance, especially the huge, rusticated stone Palazzo Pitti, found fruit in his later Marshall Field Wholesale Store. The party enjoyed side trips to Siena and Orvieto but got no closer to Rome because Richardson suffered from the intense heat. Sightseeing by day—"church and tomb, one after the other, street after street," according to his assistant—and traveling by night, they headed north through Bologna, Ravenna, and Padua, and finally arrived at Venice.

"I have been in sort of a dream land," Richardson wrote home from Venice in mid-August. The party engaged two gondolas for a week, complete with gondoliers dressed in white with broad blue collars and broad blue sashes fringed with white and gold hanging below their knees. Jacques reported that the architect "begrudged a moment's rest." They lived on their watercraft from morning to evening, letter writing, sightseeing, visiting Torcello and Murano to shop— Richardson wanted to buy the whole of Murano—or drifting through the midnight carnival on the Grand Canal, following a great barge full of music.

"You should have seen the man in Venice!" exclaimed Brooks. "The wonder is that any gondola could hold such enthusiasm and energy." They attended Mass and vespers in St. Mark's, drank coffee or "superb" orange water ice, watched the people, and listened to a band in the piazza. Jacques dreaded to see "the long 'schooners' of iced beer set before him, and order upon order for ices given at Bauer's." They studied the work of Tintoretto, presumably the celebrated cycle of frescoes in the Scuola di San Rocco. They made trips out to Padua and Verona, where San Zeno Maggiore offered an Italian contrast to the Romanesque of France and Spain. Finally all this caught up with Richardson, and he was "quite ill" for a few days. Still, Venice had filled him to the brim, according to Jacques, "and it was enchanting to see his genuine delight and almost childlike glee."

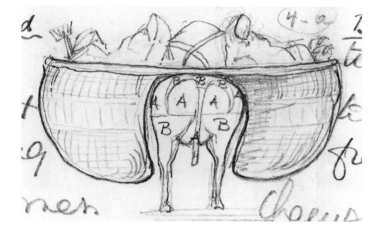

H. H. Richardson, sketch of a decoratively clipped donkey on the way to market, Catalonia, 1882. Richardson drew this vignette in a letter to his wife written during his European journey. (Printing and Graphic Arts, Houghton Library, Harvard University, Cambridge, Massachusetts)

Richardson hated to leave at the end of the week. The party crossed to Milan, where it began to break apart, with the architect and his assistant heading for Spain. Brooks, now setting course for a long sojourn in Germany, had been happy as a member of the party and would miss them, although the architects' focus seems to have finally bored him, and his summation was less than ecstatic. "Richardson is full of intelligence and cultivation in his own art," he wrote, "and Jacques is a pleasant fellow."

On the "vile" boat between Genoa and Marseilles, with the sea running high, Richardson again fell "very ill." Then the architect, his draftsman, and his "willing & good" body servant, Hiscock, rode through splendid weather from Perpignan to Barcelona along the Costa Brava on a road that hugged the cliffs overlooking the Mediterranean. The party reached its destination after midnight, with Richardson "very tired." They ate some bread and chocolate, then fell into bed. In Barcelona he relaxed, shopped, bought photographs, and ate. "I never knew what a grape was until a moment ago," he wrote. He also enjoyed the Gothic cathedral, especially the cloisters and "fine old glass." He dissembled to Julia that he felt "splendid," although he admitted to "a slight draw back" in Milan. Richardson was congenitally incapable of squarely facing his health problems: according to Jacques, it had been much more than that.

From Barcelona they traveled by train westward to Saragossa, passing through Lérida and arriving late on August 26. Knowing Julia would appreciate descriptions of people more than buildings, he discussed both in his letters. The Spanish peasants in this area of Catalonia, especially the men, dressed in brightly colored turbans, short black velvet jackets, trousers slashed and reaching the knee, broad purple sashes about the waist, long stockings, and "queer" sandals with black ribbons connecting toes and ankles. They came to market with large baskets of goods piled on their decoratively clipped donkeys. At Saragossa he attended a bullfight but, he insisted, saw only one poor "cow" killed and was "thoroughly ashamed of having stayed through such a disgusting performance."

The architect felt himself to be in a whirl, but he was trying his best to keep track of his itinerary. He proved himself a meticulously prepared student of architecture, buying and studying photographs along the way, reading before visits to buildings, reading while sightseeing, and reading again in the evening. No wonder he occasionally collapsed. He liked Saragossa cathedral, especially its "noble" interior and octagonal dome, and particularly admired its exterior walls of brick and green, black, and yellow tiles. He included in his letter a slight sketch of the arrangement, although he thought it "folly" to try to draw, given the need to hurry on. He criticized artists and photographers who did not take time to understand what they recorded. Jacques wrote that they found in Saragossa arches composed of eight-foot voussoirs. Richardson appropriated such grandly scaled details in his later work at Pittsburgh and Chicago. Not surprisingly, he thought rococo San Pilas "horrible," but as a totality the city whetted his appetite "to press on."

Like many another traveler before and since, the architect fretted about what to bring home as presents for Julia and the children, but seemed more interested in the souvenirs he had gathered for himself. He "picked up a few things at out-of-the-way places," a couple of peasant crosses that he thought were pretty and interesting "beyond their money value." In Spain photographs and books, however, accounted for most of his spending. The appointments of his library in Brookline thus became richly augmented.

Richardson, Jacques, and Hiscock left Saragossa for Zamora via a long loop southward through Madrid and Salamanca. On the train from Saragossa through Guadalajara to Madrid they crossed some "striking scenery, desolate, bold & grand," but occasionally spotted "superb peaches and great black figs" growing along the way. They passed a "curious village," Saltillas, built entirely underground—all they could see from the train were chimneys rising from the earth. The inhabitants were as dirty and forlorn, Richardson wrote, as any people he had ever imagined.

He arrived in Madrid "thoroughly worn out." The city he found uninteresting, too much like any other European capital. The travelers spent their time here watching people and visiting the galleries. The justly famous collection of old masters in the Prado made Richardson regret that he had to leave so soon. A side trip to Toledo through what Jacques reported as "excessive heat" introduced him to that "noble & big" thirteenth-century cathedral. He admired the bridge of San Martín and the nearby old Moorish gate, the Puerto del Sol. He saw more Moorish work there, the southernmost point of his Spanish visit, than anywhere else.

Casa de Doña Maria la Brava, Salamanca. Details of medieval masonry, such as the huge voussoirs composing this archway, were to inspire Richardson's designs after he returned from Europe in 1882. (Richardson Photographic Collection, Loeb Library, Harvard Graduate School of Design)

Detail of entrance arcade, Oakes Ames Memorial Hall, North Easton, Massachusetts, 1879–81. Richardson was using stumpy columns, robust capitals, and stone arches long before he visited French and Spanish Romanesque sites to reconfirm his preferences.

Back in Madrid, Richardson hired a Spanish-speaking guide named Patrick to ease their journey through the north of Spain, the second major focus of this breathtaking agenda. This area contained the greatest concentration of the country's important Romanesque monuments, but it was also territory little explored by Americans, and neither Richardson nor Jacques spoke the language. On September 1 the foursome of architect, assistant, body servant, and guide headed overnight across the hills for Salamanca via Ávila and Medina del Campo.

The architect does not mention Philip II's austere retreat at San Lorenzo del Escorial, although it stood in his way. He sought the Middle Ages, not the Renaissance. According to Jacques, the walled fortress of Ávila ranked as the "most quaint and interesting" town they visited in Spain. Richardson was "fairly overcome with delight" at the battlemented cathedral. There was much else to see, but the twelfth-century pilgrimage church of San Vicente and the richly sculpted Romanesque cloister of Santo Domingo de Silos sat high on the list. They gained access to the Dominican convent by lying: Patrick told the monks they were Catholics. In Salamanca the "simple & beautiful" old cathedral attracted his attention. The architect had adapted one of its cupolas for the tower of Trinity Church, and according to Jacques conceived his scheme for the design of the Albany cathedral here. Richardson bought a photograph showing the arched doorway of the Casa de Doña Maria la Brava with its huge dressed voussoirs. He would draw upon this inspiration too in subsequent work. In Salamanca he also met a Spanish gentleman named Emilio Nieto, who took him to a play that Nieto translated for him and to a superb ballet.

The group reached Zamora on September 3 after a forty-mile ride northward in a private diligence drawn by two horses and two mules. Hiscock and Patrick, "a thorough liar but a useful man as he spoke the language" (he once told them a train was late because the water had frozen in the boilers), rode on top with the baggage; Richardson and Jacques sat within. On the way they gnawed tough roasted chickens washed down with bottles of wine and water. Jacques said he preferred the railway cars.

They were pushing for Paris now. By the eighth they had reached Burgos, where the weather turned cold. On the broad arc northward then east from Zamora, they had stopped to climb the rickety clock tower of the Romanesque Collegiata in Toro, "once a city of considerable importance but now no better than an Irish village." This was not well-traveled territory, especially for Americans. The hotel keeper insisted that he had never met an American in seventeen years on the job, although he had seen an Englishman or two. On a side trip by train to León on September 6, Richardson had made the mistake of admiring the watch of a fellow traveler, and to his horror, "after the true old Spanish fashion," the fellow insisted he accept it as a present. He refused "as a matter of course," but vowed not to forget that custom again.

In León the cathedral and the church of San Isidoro attracted Richardson's eye, but the church of San Marcos he could not fit into his tight schedule. An attendant told them they were the first Americans to visit San Isidoro. Richardson upset the priest who showed them around when he refused the holy water offered as he entered. Still he admired much here, especially the Panteón de los Reyes, or royal burial chamber, with its massive supports, richly carved capitals, and vaults decorated in fresco during the Romanesque period, but the interior of the church itself he thought had been damaged by later work and a disagreeable color scheme. The Gothic cathedral was undergoing repairs, but the clerk of the works "very politely" showed Richardson the drawings and escorted him all over the building. In the earlier and recently discovered crypt he found the "great, fat, stumpy columns, strong, robust caps, and massive vaulting" that Jacques said he took to heart.

In Burgos, once the capital of Castile and León, he visited another "fine old" cathedral and rode out to look at two convents, the nunnery of the Huelgas, which was closed to men because it was the "retreat of noble women," and the Cartuja de Miraflores. On the way back to town he met an English clergyman who "knew all about Dr. Priestley," the architect's illustrious ancestor, "& was very polite."

After some seven cities in the previous seven days, Richardson finally confessed to Julia that the pace had left him fatigued. "I have been travelling at a fearful rate & must feel the effects of it soon" he wrote. In Spain there had been hardships as well as architecture. Still, the architect was happy as well as tired. Although the trip had been "short and hurried in the extreme," wrote Jacques, "Richardson drank his fill of the lovely eleventh-to-thirteenth century work." Only the lack of time and railroads prevented them from reaching Santiago de Compostela, in the extreme northwest of the country, the hoped-for destination of all on the Romanesque pilgrimage road.

So they continued northeast toward France, enjoying a "charming" ride through the Pyrenees to Bayonne to visit still another cathedral, then on to Poitiers. On the train near Bordeaux a woman with three children joined them in their compartment. "She nursed them, & spanked them, and fed them with greasy meat, & they did everything that children usual[ly] do & ought not to do," according to the architect. Poitiers held much of interest to Richardson. The Romanesque pile of Notre-Dame-la-Grande might have occupied his attention for a whole day except that he also wanted to visit St.-Radegonde, St.-Hilaire,

*Staircase, Robert Treat Paine house, Waltham,
Massachusetts, 1884–87. This mountain of wood
paneling, turned spindles, carved ornament, flowing
stairs, and built-in benches forms the focus of the
vast entrance hall.*

St.-Porchaine, and other religious and public works. Notre-Dame features a richly sculpted facade, and Jacques wrote that the architect "raved over carvings and details for hours."

Richardson hoped to see Amiens, Beauvais, Rouen, and Rheims, but probably did not. The travelers stayed in Paris for a week this time. The architect looked up his former classmates, especially Adolphe Gerhardt, who was now an established architect, and had long talks with them. Jacques says Richardson urged them to give up "the old cut-and-dried-course," the rigid classical method of the École, and work out their own style. He must have thought he had done just that. He "threw his whole soul" into his arguments, but had little effect. In America, perhaps, the architect could do what he wanted, they said, but in France, "public opinion was too strong and government positions too necessary." If he had not already come to that conclusion, Richardson must now have realized that he had been wise not to remain in Paris after the Civil War.

After another week in London seeing "the Doctors & my truss makers," and certainly for more socializing, on September 27, just two days before Richardson's forty-fourth birthday, he and Jacques headed homeward on the Cunarder *Cephalonia*, whose maiden voyage had occurred just a month earlier. He returned to Brookline with new knowledge of, renewed enthusiasm for, and many photographs and books devoted to monumental lithic works of French and Spanish Romanesque architecture. (A passion hardly sated—when George Shepley visited Paris a year later, he was charged with gathering still more photographs and books for the architect.) And this says nothing of his swollen collection of *objets*. On this journey he surely meant to take stock of his position, measure himself against past and contemporary European work, and recharge his creative energies. He said he wanted to see how "those old fellows" had accomplished what he was trying to do, and what he found was what he wanted to find: qualities of "simplicity and repose" in the large forms and an "exquisite refinement" in the details.

By the time of this trip Richardson ranked as a major American architect. He had to his credit a body of mature work that established his independence, creativity, and leadership. He must have returned with great hopes for the future, but he returned exhausted. To his client Mrs. Nicolas Anderson in Washington, he seemed "no better in health and even less capable of activity." His future was to occupy a mere three and a half years, but that was time enough for him to conceive many of his finest works.

9 ❖ STUDIO DAYS
1880s

IN THE EARLY 1880S RICHARDSON ACHIEVED HIS FULL PERSONA.
A series of portraits taken around 1883 by the noted photographer George Collins Cox shows his ever-expanding bulk wrapped in monk's habit complete with cowl and tasseled waist cord. Some of these photographs include his full figure; some are busts; in some he stands or sits at a carpet-covered table holding a large tome, ample beer stein at his elbow. In these photographs the architect represents himself as a jovial medieval Friar Tuck—the image the mature Richardson wished to present to the world.

The architect could have had a practical reason for this costume. The Brookline studio, the Coops, housed not only drafting areas but drafty ones as well. Such a wrap might have been most welcome there on wintry days, but no photograph shows him wearing his habit in that environment. There are many of these staged portraits, and they were carefully posed, so they must present an image the architect wanted to broadcast: that of a neomedieval master builder or preindustrial craftsman. In this he drew upon an English tradition. A.W. N. Pugin depicted a Gothic architect-monk at work in his study in the frontispiece to his *True Principles of Pointed or Christian Architecture* of 1841. The conceit reflected the thinking of the Arts and Crafts Movement spawned in England by Pugin's followers, including William Morris, a movement carried to New England by Richardson among others. Indeed, some of his former assistants ran the Boston Arts and Crafts Society in the late 1890s.

These portraits of the architect as medieval monk represent Richardson's reluctance artistically to embrace the products of the Industrial Revolution. Just as he made what was then thought to be a medieval building on the grounds of Abingdon Abbey in England the "keynote," as he said, of his design for the Glessner house in Chicago, so the medieval served as the keynote for all Richardson's work. He shared this attitude, artistically if not politically, with Pugin, Ruskin, Morris, and others who championed medieval romance over modern expediency. The idea was not to go back in time but to bring forward the best of the past to ameliorate the worst of the present.

Photographs exist of the mature architect in more fashionable dress. One appears as the frontispiece of Van Rensselaer's biography; another was taken by Clover Adams, an accomplished photographer, during a visit by Richardson to

OPPOSITE: *Detail of main entrance, J. J. Glessner house, Chicago, 1885–87. The arrangement of arch above peaked lintel was a detail new in Richardson's work, and one inspired by similar Romanesque details he had seen in the Auvergne.*

Washington. He averts his eyes in these bust-length images, which capture his center-parted dark hair, full facial beard, and puffy features but avoid emphasizing his enormous body.

For the definitive image of the man as most others saw him we must turn to the justly famous portrait painted posthumously from charcoal sketches made in December 1885 by the Anglo-Teutonic artist Sir Hubert von Herkomer. Richardson and Herkomer exchanged services, the architect providing suggestive drawings for the artist's castlelike residence outside London. Herkomer placed Richardson's huge bulk in the center of a horizontal canvas, close to the picture plane and thus to the viewer. He sits at his desk surrounded by the objects of *virtù* collected in his travels and displayed in his library. Richardson confronts the viewer directly, his shining eyes peering out from a hirsute head set atop a massive convex torso covered with a tent-sized vest and loose-fitting jacket. Herkomer later wrote that the architect at this point in his life looked "wrong when dressed up for society." Still, his body language is open, inviting, sympathetic. Herkomer presents a warm personality, the man John Hay called, with Phillips Brooks's concurrence, "as bright and genial as sunshine."

Herkomer's portrait of Richardson presents us with an image of warmth and creative energy within a massive frame. The artist wrote that the architect was "as solid in his friendships as in his figure. Big-bodied big-hearted large-minded full-brained." Herkomer's portrait reflects the prevailing attitude toward the architect, for it denies the true state of the man's health and instead shows him radiating vitality and well-being, with "character and fire in his face," according to the artist. In denying the medical truth, however, Herkomer captured a greater one, for this is the architect as his contemporaries thought of him: a creative giant among mere workaday professionals, a large and cogent presence, a "magnetic force," according to the obituary of P. B. Wight.

Richardson's warmth could be turned on and off at will, depending upon his audience. He was actor enough to create the appropriate presentation in all situations. Whereas one observer thought that the queen of Sheba herself would receive his usual hearty handshake, bright smile, and friendly word, another assistant has left another image, of "his lordship" sitting in his study, where he "puffed and snorted" behind a huge desk "heavily draped with the most expensive goods." There he presided in state "to give audience to some humble creditors" who might brave his lair to present their claims. If an unfortunate collector reached his "royal presence," he became "forthwith paralyzed by the effect of the surroundings" and convinced that another time might better serve for the payment of monies owed.

Ailments minor and major continued to shape the architect's life, and the pace of complaints about various afflictions quickened after his European journey.

Main front, J. J. Glessner house, Chicago, 1885–87. Richardson delighted in upsetting a balanced composition by extending one flank —that on the left—to generate vitality within an otherwise static design.

nomination be seconded by the president of the club, the celebrated historian Francis Parkman, who also summered in the architect's Brookline neighborhood.

As usual at social events such as the afternoon with the Listemann group, there was more on the architect's agenda than music. On a similar afternoon the next year, according to a visiting English student, "a large and fashionable assembly" not only listened to "excellent music, finely played," but had the opportunity to look at drawings and photographs of his works, both those completed and those in progress. So Richardson pushed his wares in a cultivated ambience. He understood the professional effectiveness of a colorful reputation, of an artistic social life, of presenting his accomplishments in a cultured setting. In the same spirit he published his designs in handsome portfolios filled with large collotype photographs. These portfolios presented the work in seductive detail—Trinity Church, the buildings at North Easton, Austin Hall—in a series of "Monographs on American Architecture," as if he had his finger on the national building pulse. These portfolios, like Van Rensselaer's biography, appeared in limited numbers at hefty prices to appeal to a discriminating and well-heeled audience, that is, to just the sort of people he would invite to his musicales and would court for his clients.

Both his afternoon at homes and his portfolios represented the best kind of advertising.

Richardson ran his office like a studio, or rather, like a Parisian atelier. His former assistant T. M. Clark, now teaching at the recently opened school of architecture at the Massachusetts Institute of Technology in the Back Bay, sent students over to join the team. One of them, Welles Bosworth, later recalled that "Richardson's huge bulk seemed to fill the entire office. His personality was so overpowering that the atmosphere was charged with it, and we all held our breaths when he came round for his morning visits to each table." All accounts stress the educational aspects of the work, and none more so than that of Mariana Van Rensselaer, who discussed the office under the heading "Methods of Teaching." Richardson owned one of the best reference libraries around and, especially after his European trip in 1882, the best collection of photographs as well. He was now a *patron* in his own right. One observer called his treatment of his helpers "courtesy itself." He seemed like a father, according to one of them, "and held them to him by the cords of personal affection as well as of professional admiration and respect."

Service entrance of the J. J. Glessner house, Chicago, 1885–87. The essence of some of Richardson's finest mature work is in his unvexed use of simple geometry, natural materials, and weighty shapes.

The architect was, according to Van Rensselaer, a born teacher as well as leader. His criticism made the office into a school. In New York and Brookline, Richardson turned out some of the leading architects of the next generation. The most important, of course, were Charles F. McKim and Stanford White. With William Rutherford Mead holding them apart and therefore together, they established the firm of McKim, Mead and White in the late 1870s, a firm that became one of the largest and certainly the most influential office of the next generation. Beginning in the late 1880s with the Boston Public Library, erected on Copley Square directly facing Trinity Church, the firm turned out the principal monumental classical works of the City Beautiful Movement in American urban planning, including Columbia University, the former Pennsylvania Station, and the turn-of-the-century Madison Square Garden—in whose rooftop restaurant Harry Thaw, enraged over the architect's affair with his wife, gunned down Stanford White in 1906. McKim, Mead and White's practice was nationwide and included the Rhode Island State Capitol, additions to Thomas Jefferson's University of Virginia, Boston's Symphony Hall, the Institute of Art in Minneapolis, and various mansions on Long Island, along the Hudson, in the Berkshires, and elsewhere.

If McKim and White headed the list, other assistants later produced works of major significance. Alexander W. Longfellow, nephew of the poet, headed Longfellow, Alden & Harlow, a firm whose work spanned between Boston and Pittsburgh, where it turned out a number of buildings for Andrew Carnegie. Herbert Langford Warren founded the school of architecture at Harvard. John Galen Howard directed a major practice and became head of architectural studies at the University of California at Berkeley. Welles Bosworth designed M.I.T.'s Cam-

Exterior, J. J. Glessner house, Chicago, 1885–87. The house presents a stern face to the public streets while harboring a protected courtyard and warm interiors.

bridge campus. Robert D. Andrews and Herbert Jacques were principals in the distinguished Boston firm of Andrews, Jacques and Rantoul. And there were, finally, the three men who succeeded to Richardson's practice: George Shepley, Charles Rutan, and Charles Coolidge.

Henry Irving, the noted British Shakespearean actor who visited Richardson during these years, thought that the architect's real legacy would not be his buildings—as great as they were in Irving's opinion—but his "work for the nation in the school which he was founding by gathering round his own studio the young men of bright promise whom he saw, and whose ability was being moulded to high endeavors by his enthusiasm." The architect's style proved transient, but his attitude toward his profession did last. Although Richardson's followers carried on his Romanesque work for only about a decade after his death, they continued throughout their careers to practice architecture as high public art according to the attitude he had fostered in them.

Irving spent an afternoon with Richardson in Brookline during this period and was struck by his "great energy and grandness of purpose." Richardson's Brookline studio recalled not only the ateliers of Paris but the workshops of the Middle Ages. It anticipated the similar paternalistic studios, based upon pre-industrial ideals, at Elbert Hubbard's Roycroft shop at East Aurora, New York, and Frank Lloyd Wright's home-studio in Oak Park, Illinois (as well as his later Taliesin studios).

All work and no play probably made bad architecture, or so Richardson seemed to think. And so he welcomed draftsmen to his family dining table on Monday evenings. They were also free to browse the library and photo collection in their off hours, or take long walks along shaded paths in the surrounding picturesque landscape. They played ball, lawn tennis, quoits. And they indulged in the usual antics of imaginative young men at ease. On one memorable occasion someone found one of Richardson's huge vests lying about in his absence and immediately discovered that it enveloped three average-sized assistants, who "in lockstep paraded the field for the edification of twenty or thirty jolly workers."

These assistants formed part of his extended family, with home life and studio life interlocked. Van Rensselaer bears witness to the fact that the architect's draftsmen "were constantly at his hearth and table."

Much of what we hear about Richardson's office comes from reminiscences meant for publication, and they are uniformly positive in their descriptions of the relationship between the master and his assistants. There were good historical reasons for painting him in bright colors, for making him the nearly flawless founder of an American school. But nobody's perfect. From the private comments of at least one of his helpers arises a slightly different picture. Alexander Wadsworth Longfellow joined the office fresh out of the École des Beaux-Arts at the beginning of 1882. As the only École-trained architect in the studio other than Richardson himself, he initially held a place of prime importance, and his privately written comments were admiring. He described Richardson as an imaginative designer who "sees things in his mind" and never forgets the details, the "small work." And, Longfellow went on, "he takes hold of his clients and makes them do the right things." But Longfellow was a classicist who eventually found Richardson's Romanesque-inspired work trying, and he became increasingly alienated. "I almost dread it," he wrote of the architect's most mature work. He found fault as well with Norcross's role in the design process, convinced that the architect should exercise greater control at the building site and not leave so much of the "office drawing" in the hands of the contractor. And finally, he abhorred the competitiveness engendered within the drafting rooms, a holdover from the Parisian atelier system.

Some of this is symptomatic of a case of envy. The criticism about competition stemmed from Longfellow's jealousy of Charles Coolidge, a more recently arrived and gifted designer who was put over his head. Richardson, he noted, made Coolidge his favorite and hoped to keep him longer than he would keep Longfellow. At this the architect lost Longfellow's allegiance. "Richardson is a strange mixture of greatness and smallness," he wrote in March 1885, "and I am heartily sick of him, he is too selfish to live and I could not stand it any longer."

The disgruntled Longfellow seems to have been something of an exception; indeed, most of Richardson's assistants remained as loyal to his memory as they had been to him. Longfellow was right in one respect, however—Richardson did have his favorites among his lieutenants. And in the case of George Shepley, the relationship became indispensable. During the mid-1880s Shepley traveled the Midwest from Cincinnati to St. Louis and Chicago, supervising the execution of the designs that issued from the Brookline Coops. In March 1886 Richardson gave him a raise in annual salary to $3,000 because he had become important in supervising distant projects, and greeted him as Jula Richardson's fiancé.

In the 1880s Richardson towered like a monadnock over the architectural world. His reputation and his commissions spread outward from New England to

Main hall, J. J. Glessner house, Chicago, 1885–87. The core of a Richardson house was the central hall, with its beamed ceiling, warming fireplace, and ample stairway sweeping up to the private rooms above.

embrace the East Coast as far as Washington, D.C., the South as far as his native New Orleans, and the Midwest from Pittsburgh to St. Louis, from Cincinnati to Chicago, with one design, the Ames Monument, erected in the far West, between Cheyenne and Laramie, in Wyoming. His old friends did not desert him, and indeed his circle of clients expanded from his Harvard ties to prominent businessmen and other leaders attracted by his reputation and achievements rather than his connections. These were leading businessmen like Marshall Field and John J. Glessner of Chicago, Frederick Billings of Vermont, Erastus Corning of Albany, and Henry S. Potter and John R. Lionberger of St. Louis. His work now habitually received notice in the national architectural press and inspired frequent imitation and emulation across the country. Many years later his Harvard College classmate the Pittsburgh lawyer, businessman, and civic leader John H. Ricketson described Richardson's influence as "everywhere to be seen and with one accord the architects of the country acknowledge his supremacy and bow before his genius."

His first major effort after returning from Europe resulted in failure to gain a commission but nonetheless produced a series of presentation drawings that, when later published, still enhanced his stature in the architectural world. The story of the failure tells us much about the architect's attitude toward clients. During his trip abroad, Richardson received a letter from William Croswell Doane, Episcopal bishop of Albany, New York, asking him to compete with one other architect for the design of a new cathedral in the capital city. Doane enlisted an Episcopal minister, Charles Babcock, who was also an architect, as his advisor. Babcock had been trained by Richard Upjohn, a man who favored Gothic for ecclesiastical work; Gothic had been the style of choice among Anglicans since the ecclesiastical reform movement of the 1840s; and the terms of the competition required Gothic as the style of the new cathedral.

Richardson chose to ignore all this and envisioned in a series of splendid presentation drawings a costly church modeled on the Romanesque architecture of the Auvergne region he had so recently admired. For windows and other openings he did use "transitional," or slightly pointed, early Gothic, forms, but he admitted that, had he built the building, he would have rounded those arches as well. Richardson knew how to sway most of his clients, but he sometimes misunderstood the role of consultants, believing that they were impartial when all the signs indicated that they had an agenda. That, plus the familiar fact that his cathedral design looked too expensive, led to its rejection. Richardson's vacillating Romanesque-cum-Gothic project lost to a real Gothic design by an English-born Albany architect named Robert C. Gibson.

Dining-room fireplace, J. J. Glessner house, Chicago, 1885–87. Broad horizontal proportions were a hallmark of Richardson's work, and they can be found here in the doorway, fireplace, paneling, and the shape of the room itself.

The architect stamped the presentation drawings for the Albany cathedral project with a red wax seal bearing his monogram, the first use of a device he had had made during his trip abroad. He wrote from London to Julia that he thought of having a seal made with his monogram surrounded by "a serpent biting its own tail." This, a symbol of eternity first used by the Egyptians, in the Renaissance appeared in a variety of emblems, in which its meaning ranged from immortality to renewal. It is impossible to know where Richardson got his idea or what precisely he intended by it, although it might be worth noting that some books contain emblems that link eternity to fame, using the device as part of an illustration of the motto *Durch Kunst erlangt man ewig Gerücht* (Through art one attains eternal fame).

Such a meaning would certainly have appealed to the architect, but he did not finally choose the motif of the snake biting its tail. Richardson returned to the topic of the seal in a later letter from Spain. His monogram remained central, but the serpent had now become "two strange beasts" who are "both biting at a piece of forbidden fruit. . . . I call it forbidden—it may not be," he added enigmatically. The beasts in Richardson's tiny sketch are serpentlike if not actually serpents. He has clearly changed the meaning of the seal from its earlier design, although his source and his intention remain uncertain. The combination of snake and forbidden fruit usually refers to the fall of man, Adam and Eve's eating of the fruit of the Tree of Knowledge of Good and Evil, but there are two snakes now, one more than called for in the book of Genesis—and why the curious qualification about whether the fruit is forbidden? We are left wondering about the architect's message. A few of his buildings from this era, Austin Hall at Harvard and the county buildings in Pittsburgh, for example, incorporate his monogram, and some of the

Library, J. J. Glessner house, Chicago, 1885–87. Furniture and appointments by Richardson's assistant Charles A. Coolidge, William Morris, and Frances Glessner created an Arts and Crafts ambience within the preindustrial architectural envelope.

drawings from his office that postdate his European trip, such as those for the Albany cathedral, bear the second design stamped in red wax.

Richardson continued to turn out railroad stations for the Boston & Albany and other lines. The largest of these was the brick Union Station at New London, Connecticut, on the exterior a reprise of Sever Hall, a project that entered the office in the fall of 1885 and remained unfinished at Richardson's death. He also continued to turn out libraries, including his largest, that for the University of Vermont at Burlington. In 1881 Frederick Billings, recently retired president of the Northern Pacific Railway (after whom Billings, Montana, is named), acquired the twelve-thousand-volume library of the late George Perkins Marsh, congressman, diplomat, conservationist, and scholar, and offered to donate the collection and a building to house it to his alma mater. Billings selected the architect after inspecting his earlier libraries and took an active interest in the design process. The result was an enlarged adaptation of Richardson's previous schemes.

As with other commissions during these years, surviving correspondence between the architect and client reveals much about their relationship and the design process. In this case a third figure, that of Matthew H. Buckham, president of the university, must also be recognized. Billings admired Richardson's Winn Memorial Library in Woburn, Massachusetts, and asked the architect to submit a sketch for Vermont. In May 1883 he wrote to Buckham suggesting some changes in this early design but added that employing Richardson was "really the proper thing to do." The architect's attitude toward clients and budgets must have become common knowledge by then, for Billings adds a cautionary note. "If you think you can control Richardson I am inclined to a meeting with him." The response to this challenge is a case study of the mature architect's way with clients.

In meetings and in subsequent correspondence, Richardson fought off suggestions for changes in his designs and lectured the impatient Billings about his proper role as patron. The architect was now a master at suggesting the artistic nature of his work and the consequent need for employers to cut him much slack. In July he wrote to Billings that there was no cause to feel uneasy about the progress of the design.

> I have from the first given the best part of my time and attention and my most careful thought to your building, and I have and shall urge the drawings along with as much rapidity as is consistent with good work. As I explained to Mr Buckham . . . the work up to July 5th was purely a matter of design, which could not be unduly hurried without serious det-

riment to the building as a work of art. Only I myself and one or two of my best draftsmen could be employed in that work.

The building as a work of art: that's where the money went; that's why budgets were busted. And Richardson's uneconomical method of working also suggests one reason for his own insolvency. Efficiency and economy were not concepts at home in the Brookline studio.

After the architect had explained his creative and laborious method of working on the library to Billings, like a patient teacher instructing a pupil he proceeded to go from the specific to the general:

I consider one of the chief reasons why there is so much bad architecture in the country is the overhaste in making the designs. We are too impatient to be willing to give the time and thought and careful reconsideration which is essential to the production of a work of art. But it were surely unwise to mar the design of a monument which is to last we hope for centuries for the sake of beginning work a week or two earlier.

Exterior of Oakes Ames Memorial Hall, North Easton, Massachusetts, 1879–81. Richardson was never to embrace the industrial esthetic that preoccupied many other nineteenth-century architects.

As he did as early as his very first building, the Church of the Unity in Springfield, Richardson again enlisted to his cause the spirit of Ruskin's Lamp of Sacrifice—the client's sacrifice. Like a fox inviting a hen to supper in his lair, the architect then asked Billings to come to Brookline so that he might show him the "careful and painstaking way in which I study and restudy a design." In meetings and as a result of such letters, Richardson found Billings a responsive student, for the donor increased his initial gift of $85,000 to a total cost of $150,000. As we shall see, John Glessner received the same Richardsonian treatment a few years later.

Richardson not only instructed individual clients on individual jobs. In his last years he had printed a broadside to explain to them his fee schedule, his responsibilities, and his relationship to the commission. This self-assured document also contained something of a declaration of artistic independence, of Emersonian self-reliance, an attitude new but not unique in the history of American architecture. In preparing a design, he wrote,

> I agree, after consultation with the owner, to use my best judgment. I cannot, however, guarantee that the building, when completed, shall conform to his ideas of beauty or taste, or indeed to those of any person or school. I can only agree to examine and consider this matter well and carefully, and to recommend nothing which is inconsistent with my own ideas upon these subjects. Of course, when I follow the owner's positive instructions, I consider myself relieved from all responsibility whatsoever.

Like all the superstar architects who followed in his wake, Richardson here asserted the proper pecking order: the client existed to provide him with funds to follow his own muse. Like those who commissioned houses of his illustrious successor Frank Lloyd Wright, Richardson's clients were forewarned that it made no difference who was paying the bills, they were to get a signature work, a "Richardson" building, which at times he even "signed" with his monogram. In the case of neither Richardson nor Wright could a client hope for the kind of control Frederick Billings had initially wanted at the Vermont library.

The architect's circular for potential clients declared his independent stance within the profession, and the design of the Vermont library exemplified his singular reaction to the introduction of industrial materials and processes into the architecture of his day. He ignored them. An architect of almost the same age and social background and of similar professional education as Richardson, Philadelphia's Frank Furness, dramatically exposed iron structural beams in the apsidal reading room of the library for the University of Pennsylvania he designed just after Richardson's work in Vermont. He gave these metallic members architectural expression following the suggestions for an Industrial Age style expounded by Viollet-le-Duc in his *Entretiens*, or lectures, on architecture. Richardson also owned Viollet's book, but he chose tradition over innovation, Ruskin over Viollet, in creating in an early sketch for the Vermont library a historically oriented interior using timber arcades supporting a series of arched timber trusses, which in turn support the roof. He eventually constructed a variant but equally conservative space using wooden beams holding up a flat ceiling. Furness used an up-to-date metal stack system for book storage; Richardson continued to use a traditional arrangement of alcoves. Furness's work reflected the industrial present by exhibiting a machine aesthetic. Richardson's reflected the preindustrial past; he created an architecture of memory.

As work piled up and as one similar program followed the other, Richardson became increasingly imposed upon by his physical ills, and confusion began to creep into the office. In March 1886, a month before he died, he wrote to his assistant George Shepley that he felt "very tired" and found it "not surprising we should now & then mix up libraries when we are building so many." He referred to an error in the specifications for his design for a library in East Saginaw, Michigan, a design prepared for a competition.

The East Saginaw library was to be built with a $100,000 bequest from Jesse Hoyt, a wealthy developer, but the consultant was William Frederick Poole, then head of the Chicago Public Library and soon to lead the American Library Association. Poole outspokenly advocated economical, flexible, utilitarian library design. The ALA had been editorializing against Richardson's landmark libraries since its inception, in the mid-1870s, so the architect showed little wisdom in assuming that Poole's "recommendations were suggestions." He made the same mistake here that he had made earlier in the competition for the Albany cathedral, when he entered a Romanesque project even though the requirements clearly called for a Gothic design. Poole was no malleable client to be flattered into spending more than he wanted for a building he had not envisioned. In Richardson's misreading of his judge at East Saginaw, he lost that commission too. The library was erected from designs of a competitor who did listen to Poole. But business abhors waste; conservation is a key to income. After Richardson's death his successors reworked the East Saginaw scheme for the Howard Library in Richardson's native New Orleans.

Lost commissions like the Albany cathedral and the East Saginaw library were rare at the height of Richardson's career. In the last years of his life the architect for the most part enjoyed the support of his clients as he turned out one major work after another, works ranging from domestic designs for city and suburb to major buildings for government and commerce. With Trinity Church and buildings in North Easton, these works had a major influence on American architecture. These are the works upon which his lasting reputation rests.

10 ❖ LAST WORKS 1882–86

"THE YOUTH GETS TOGETHER HIS MATERIALS TO BUILD A BRIDGE TO the moon, or perchance a palace or temple on the earth, and at length the middle-aged man concludes to build a wood-shed with them," wrote Richardson's older Massachusetts contemporary Henry David Thoreau. This metaphor of lost ambition or lack of achievement applies to most of us, no doubt, but its message is not actually true of any architect, and especially not the successful, the gifted, the signature architect. By what is usually thought of as middle age, Richardson had built impressive homes, a breathtakingly beautiful church, and many other memorable buildings. But what is usually thought of as the middle was to Richardson the end.

He must have sensed this. What we might see as his self-destructive habits perhaps originated in a fatalistic attitude toward life and death that may have stemmed from his father's early demise. Rather than conserve himself and perhaps extend his life, Richardson unwisely drove himself all the harder so that he might achieve as much as he could in the time allotted. "Such was his love for . . . architecture," we read in one of his obituaries, "that often he has risen from his sick-bed to visit his works." On the other hand, P. B. Wight believed that without his work he would not have lived as long as he did. As his health declined, the quality of that work increased. His mid-forties were his most productive years, and his last.

In these years the architect designed for a number of affluent clients a series of urban, suburban, and country houses that continued the domestic accomplishments of his earlier days. Among the finest of these were the Hay and Adams houses in Washington, the Robert Treat Paine house in Waltham, Massachusetts, the E. W. Gurney house at Pride's Crossing on the North Shore of Boston, all begun in 1884, along with the Henry S. Potter house in St. Louis and the John J. Glessner house in Chicago, begun in 1885. These continued to demonstrate Richardson's adaptation of his designs to specific environmental zones ranging from city to suburb to countryside.

The contiguous Hay and Adams dwellings located across Lafayette Square from the White house were designed for prominent clients who were the architect's exact contemporaries. John Hay, Henry Adams, and their wives had been close friends for several years. In his varied career Hay served as private secretary

OPPOSITE: *Courtyard of the Allegheny County Courthouse, Pittsburgh, 1883–88. Richardson's interest in the earlier granite architecture of New Orleans and Boston underlay his own signature use of monumental rugged stonework.*

to President Lincoln, worked as an editorial writer for the *New York Tribune*, held the post of assistant secretary of state, and wrote poetry, novels, and history. He later served as secretary of state under Presidents McKinley and Roosevelt and authored the Open Door Policy with China. Descendant of presidents, Henry Adams had known Richardson since college days and had published a novel, *Esther*, whose setting was the decoration of Boston's Trinity Church. A historian and famed autobiographer, he abandoned teaching at Harvard to move to Washington to research and write, although it was also said that he wanted to keep an eye on the White house, home to his ancestors. His study of French architecture of the Middle Ages, published in 1904 as the classic *Mont-Saint-Michel and Chartres*, resulted, he said, from a "disease" he had caught from "dear old Richardson, who was the only really big man I ever knew." Since he had known Phillips Brooks and other men who physically dwarfed the architect, he was not referring merely to size.

Neither Hay nor Adams lacked resources, although Hay was the richer of the two and the Hay house was accordingly the larger of the pair. Hay seems to have been a docile client. Henry and his wife, Marian "Clover" Adams, were anything but, and surviving correspondence shows them often at loggerheads—at least epistolary loggerheads—with their "Richelaisian" friend, the "Brookline titan . . . [who] devours men crude, and shows the effects of inevitable indigestion in his size." The flippant attitude toward the architect's physical condition is noteworthy. How much of this sort of thing was mere verbal jousting it is difficult to say, given Adams's chronic ambivalence and the factitious tone of the banter, but as usual Richardson wanted to spend more of his clients' money than they did, and that led to a great deal of complaint.

At the time that Hay signed contracts for his house he wrote to Adams that "Richardson is to tell me, if he ever finds out, 1st What we are to have and 2d What it is to cost." Adams, on the other hand, guarded against the architect's habit of producing designs "which economy itself could not resist," and he and Clover actively tried to apply some budgetary brakes and have some say in the appearance of their house. Richardson seemed up to the challenge. In February 1884 he wrote to Adams: "Your liking Hay's house better than your own is accounted for easily I think by the fact that in designing the former I was left entirely untrammelled by restrictions wise or otherwise (How's that old boy—couldn't help it—too good to pass)." But he did add that he did not despair "of making your house *at least* as attractive as Hay's and saving *all* your pet notions also."

In Adams Richardson may have met his match, and the client for once may have had the last laugh. By early 1884 both Hay and Adams had prepared or had had prepared their own scaled plans for their houses and sent them off to Richardson for "improvement." There is reason to believe that Adams drew his with one

H. H. Richardson, hall of the John Hay house, Washington, D.C., 1884–86. The clarity and sweep of this now-demolished interior set it apart from the clutter of most late-nineteenth-century interior design.

eye on plates in Viollet-le-Duc's publications. As a student Richardson had acquired the Frenchman's books, and in at least one instance, about 1870, he copied a tower from Viollet, but as a student he had also publicly demonstrated his dislike for the Gothicist's teaching, and his opinion in 1885 had not changed. P. B. Wight was wrong to assert that Richardson became a brilliant exponent of Viollet-le-Duc's views; the Gothicist remained in his mind "an archaeologist—a theorist—never an architect." Nevertheless, Richardson's revisions of Adams's design never quite eliminated the pet Ducian "notions" Adams set into his facade, despite the fact he thought that the depth to which Adams "must have fallen in quoting him as an authority on design is painful."

Although both were urbane domiciles, the Hay and Adams houses were an ill-matched pair. The visitor entered the larger Hay house through a signature low-sprung archway off Sixteenth Street, which gave access to a broad, exquisitely paneled hall with fireplace and sweeping stairway. From this central point one could reach the formal library, parlor, dining, and reception rooms on the ground floor, or the private rooms upstairs. The exterior rose brick above a stone base and looked rather severe in its restricted use of ornament. Only plain towers, gables, or molded chimneys enlivened the block. It turned the corner onto H Street, where the smaller Adams house faced Lafayette Square between party walls. The architect opened the stone base of the Adams house with paired segmental arches delicately carved. Above this rose a rather plain three-story brick wall with deeply recessed windows symmetrically arranged. Both houses were demolished in the 1920s to make way for the Hay-Adams Hotel, although some decorative fragments of the Adams arches survive in the front of a suburban house.

While he was struggling to maintain control of the Adams house in Washington, Richardson also designed a very different house on the shore at Pride's

Terrace front of the Robert Treat Paine house, Waltham, Massachusetts, 1884–87. The towers and lower walls of the Paine house are constructed of the same rude boulders Richardson often used when he designed for rural settings.

Crossing, Massachusetts, for Clover Adams's sister Ellen and her husband, Dean Ephram W. Gurney of Harvard. Erected on a site rising above the sea on a barren granite ledge, the Gurney house suggests an extension of the natural landscape. It is a composition of sloping roofs and sturdy walls of locally quarried granite slabs, devoid of historical architectural references but laid up "with their moss on," according to the local newspaper. Another of the architect's geological analogies, it survives as altered.

The Adams and Gurney houses differed radically: the one an urbane city dwelling and the other its rustic country in-law. The contrast demonstrated Richardson's Olmsted-influenced control over environmentally differentiated design. The two had one sad note in common, however, for in each case one of the clients did not live to enjoy the house. Clover Adams committed suicide in December

Exterior, Robert Treat Paine house, Waltham, Massachusetts, 1884–87. The house rises out of Frederick Law Olmsted's landscape and terrace as a natural extension of the rolling picturesque site.

1885, while her brother-in-law Ephram Gurney died of heart disease in September 1886. Dean Gurney was fifty-seven; Clover Adams, just forty-three. Nor does that end the necrology associated with these related houses, for the architect himself died in April 1886, and eventually Ellen Gurney herself would end her own life. Then the tragic circle closed. Richardson himself unwittingly composed a sad epitaph just after Clover's death. "What a different end to what we all looked forward to," he wrote to Henry Adams.

Another of Richardson's geologically inspired late domestic designs formed a huge addition to an existing midcentury house, conceived for Robert Treat Paine in Waltham, Massachusetts. The architect had worked with this client before, at Trinity Church. A year older than Richardson, Paine graduated from Harvard in 1855. Although admitted to the bar, he married well, invested wisely, and spent his life in philanthropic causes. In the 1860s he built a mansarded summer home near that of his father-in-law, Theodore Lyman. Lyman's was a Federal Palladian house, known as the Vale, designed in the early years of the nation by Salem's famed Samuel McIntire. In 1883 Paine asked Richardson to move his earlier house and extend it with a huge living and sleeping wing. He would call the result Stonehurst. The architect and Olmsted established the new site in the fall of 1884 on a high ridge looking southeast from its rolling topography. Olmsted designed the terrace, shaped by low serpentine walls of glacial boulders. These sweep up into Richardson's asymmetrical offset towers, where the natural granite stones are contrasted with window heads, jambs, and sills of roughly split slabs of red sandstone. Towers and terrace weld house to ground—or rather, the house seems to emerge from its elevated site as an earthy incident in the rugged landscape. The pinched proportions of the original mansarded house recalled Richardson's early residence on Staten Island; the broad sweep of the seemingly

nature-made addition measured the vast distance he had traveled as a designer in less than two decades.

Once above the ground, some of the exterior walls of the Paine house become wood-shingled surfaces. This combination of stone and wood—undressed stone and unpainted wood—enhances the effect of the house as an object occurring naturally in the landscape, at one with its environment. But Richardson enriched the architectural message by the use of contrast: he applied a sophisticated icon from the history of classical architecture in the center of the frontal gable. Above the boulder arch that seems to echo a natural bridge, he affixed to the shingle wall a Palladian window, a ubiquitous feature of Anglo-American Colonial and Early Republican architecture. It fronts nothing but a closet at the end of the upstairs corridor and so appears to function only as an identifying sign. If the geological aspects of the design create a sense of timeless continuity between house and site, this emblem suggests another continuity, a dynastic chain linking Paine to his in-laws in the neoclassical Vale at the bottom of the hill as well as to his own illustrious forebear, the Robert Treat Paine who had signed the Declaration of Independence in 1776. Richardson created here an architectural assertion of Paine's long-established place and distinguished ancestry; again he created an architecture of memory.

The visitor to Stonehurst discovers the most breathtaking aspect of the house not on the exterior but in the interior. The central living hall—its vast uncluttered expanse achieved by hanging the main beam from the roof truss rather than supporting it with a freestanding column—is the culminating domestic space of Richardson's career, the descendant of those halls he had begun to adapt from English practice early in the previous decade. Anchored by a huge fireplace of the richest marble and a massive wooden staircase enhanced with built-in seating, turned spindles, and carved ornament, this room is made even more impressive by its beamed and gold-leafed ceiling, deep red walls dotted with stenciled Japanese patterns above a paneled dado, cozy nooks, and exotic bric-a-brac. It effectively projected the sense of deep-seated worth assumed by its Brahmin owners.

The Henry Potter house in St. Louis, designed early in 1886 for a prominent businessman connected by marriage to George Shepley, was the architect's definitive work in the suburban Shingle style. The plan assumed an L shape (including the stables), its thin linear residential arm articulated by offset cross axes marking the hall with fireplace and stair toward the street, and dining room with fireplace toward the rear. This room bulged into the garden and reflected in plan the semicircular shape of the stair tower in front. At the end of this wing the parlor drew light through windows overlooking a three-sided veranda. The interior must have been flooded with daylight.

On the exterior the house was shaped by simplicity itself, with the long horizontal of the residential wing opposed by the cylindrical stair tower, and the surfaces continuously covered by shingles from ground line to roof ridge. The house was subsequently the residence of E. J. Russell, a prominent architect associated with the St. Louis office of Richardson's successors. When he willed it to the city, in 1958, it was demolished to create a small park on the site.

The John J. Glessner house of 1885 on modish Prairie Avenue in South Side Chicago forms a sharp contrast to the Paine and Potter houses. It stands as the definitive urban domestic design of Richardson's last years. The architect and his clients, like the architect and his builder, seem ill matched. Glessner, five years younger than Richardson, was vice president of a manufacturer of agricultural machinery that later merged into International Harvester. Small, wiry, a teetotaler, he looked upon Richardson with awe and upon his habits with some disapproval. In a memoir written thirty years later, Glessner put the architect's weight at 370 pounds. While that may have been a bit of an exaggeration, it may also suggest that he, like so many others, saw Richardson as much larger than life. He did say that the architect was the "most dominating" person he had ever seen. Richardson was "inclined to be lawless about social conventions," Glessner wrote, ate "what he liked in defiance of doctors, [and] work[ed] when he ought not." His dress seemed "a little raw" to this orthodox businessman, but "harmonious and picturesque" and ultimately "suitable *for him*." The Herkomer portrait does suggest that, at the top of his corpulence, late in life, Richardson abandoned Savile Row fashion for more comfortable, perhaps more "artistic" dress.

John Glessner's wife, Frances, was an accomplished silversmith, and the couple were supporters not only of such local cultural institutions as the Chicago Symphony Orchestra but of the ideals of the English and American Arts and Crafts Movement as well. The Glessners and Richardson worked harmoniously together, despite the fact that Frances Glessner was not overly taken with the architect's personality. In an apparently typical female reaction to this well-padded and clubby male, she called him the largest person she had ever seen, one who "stutters and sputters [and] breathes very heavy," and "aside from his profession . . . not what I should call an interesting man."

The architect sketched the Glessner plan over supper in Chicago. The design matured in Brookline in Richardson's upstairs bedroom and in the sprawling Coops. The clients visited Cottage Street during trips to their summer place in New Hampshire. They had invited Richardson to visit them there, but the

Main hall of the Robert Treat Paine house, Waltham, Massachusetts, 1884–87. Richardson's most impressive domestic interior is this vast living hall containing an uncluttered sweep of space from the marble fireplace on the left to the mountainous staircase on the right.

architect would have none of that. As he did with Frederick Billings and other clients, Richardson beckoned the Glessners to his Brookline lair. "I have been carefully considering your whole scheme," he wrote, "and would like very much to . . . talk it over with you here where I could refer . . . to different building materials—photographs—books &c." He was very busy with other work, he said, but begged to assure them "that no work interests me more than your house." No doubt he said the same to each of his clients. Materials, photographs, books, and the setting itself, all were there to assist in the seduction. As Welles Bosworth wrote, "Who could resist such a man, especially in this overpowering environment?" It was a sentiment echoed often by those who visited Richardson's illustrious successor Frank Lloyd Wright in his own dens in Wisconsin and Arizona.

The entire Glessner family came for lunch on Sunday, September 27, 1885, two days before Richardson's forty-seventh birthday. They chatted in the entry hall with daughters Jula and Mary until the man himself, who must have watched them approach from the windows of his cork-lined bedroom, appeared via the latticed and amber-lighted stairway and swept them through the house and into the studio. In the drafting room Richardson lifted a cover to unveil a "most beautifully drawn" second-floor plan for their house. When Frances Glessner complained about closets, Richardson summarily canceled the drawing. The clients

went away feeling sorry for the draftsman, who would have to do it all over again. Like everyone else, John Glessner liked best the library beyond the Coops—the fireplace, the massive desk, the cracks, or "checks," in the overhead beams. "God Almighty made those checks," the architect had told his builder. "Don't you dare to fill them up."

The following day the clients and their architect lunched in Boston, then toured Trinity Church and its rectory. Richardson thought he could improve on the design of the church if he had the chance to do it over. Sitting with his clients in that grand interior, he cleverly implied that they were to get the work of a better architect. When Glessner commented on the unusually broad doors in the rectory, the architect spouted no ponderous architectural theory but simply explained that he had designed them "so my friend Brooks and I can walk through together arm in arm."

Later, at tea back at the home-studio, Glessner wondered why Richardson lived in Brookline, so far from the center of bustling Boston. His answer came when Francis Parkman dropped by to gossip lightheartedly about a recent meeting of the convivial Saturday Club. Parkman, famous as the author of *The Oregon Trail*, summered on Jamaica Pond near the foot of Cottage Street. A man crippled by even more ailments than the architect, he had probably climbed the hill supported by his heavy canes. The famed historian and man of letters belonged to the Boston patrician class, which viewed itself as the custodian of culture, a class from which Richardson drew his professional chores and borrowed his social standing. "That's why I like to live in Brookline," Richardson said to Glessner when Parkman departed.

That evening they dined at the Country Club, despite the fact that it had been reserved for a banquet honoring some English cricket players. "Imperious" Richardson would not take no for an answer to his request for a table. After a "very good" meal he sent the Glessners, no doubt with spinning heads, back to their hotel with a pair of photographs of himself. The celebrity architect.

This genial association of architect and clients produced one of Richardson's finest houses and an American domestic masterpiece, although not a design that was liked by everyone. Compared to the other houses on Prairie Avenue in Chicago, such as the mansarded French château Richard Morris Hunt had designed for Marshall Field in the previous decade, on the exterior the Glessner house seems an austere granite fortress. The public stonework is a monochromatic layered ashlar that forms continuous horizontal lines binding the walls into a unit. The Prairie Avenue facade plays symmetry against asymmetry. The design of the main entrance follows that of openings Richardson had admired in the Auvergne, while the service entrance around the corner is a composition of huge granite voussoirs and unvexed geometry of a kind he had studied in Spain. The exterior displays little ornament to detract from the impact of the whole. The Glessners' neighbors hated their views of the house; the critic Montgomery Schuyler called it defensible only in a military sense; a young Frank Lloyd Wright drew inspiration from it.

The L-shaped plan presents a nearly solid exterior to the corner of Eighteenth Street and Prairie Avenue but opens up into a more relaxed, domestically scaled inner courtyard. In contrast to the formality of the outer facades, the courtyard becomes relatively informal, with walls, bay, and turrets of brick trimmed in rough-faced stone that respond to the inner needs of the plan. The architecture is appropriately unbuttoned in this private family space, in contrast to the starched shirtfront of the public walls.

The main floor of the house is up one level from the street. The broad paneled entrance hall contains a welcoming fireplace and an inviting stairway. The hall leads to the study, at the corner, and to the dining room, behind the chimney. Light pours in through the large windows set into the courtyard walls. Hardware, furniture, carpets, and other decorative arts were all wrought in the spirit of the Arts and Crafts Movement, some designed by Richardson's office, some purchased from William Morris's shops, some made by Frances Glessner herself. Despite the reactions of their more conventional neighbors, John and Frances Glessner were well satisfied with Richardson's house: she thought it "truly beautiful and in every way desirable and delightful"; he wrote much later that of all Richardson's works, this is the one he "would have liked most to live in." The house stands splendidly preserved, open to the public, and one of the major monuments of American domestic architecture.

During Richardson's stay in Chicago, while the Glessner house and the Field Store were in the planning stages, he wrote several letters to his oldest son, sixteen-year-old John Cole Hayden, or Hayd. These contain the kind of timeworn parental observations that try the patience of eager offspring. In one the father praised his son's last letter "because it was natural bordering as it does on impudence and conceit." Hayd had had some calling cards printed on which he added "Mr." to his name; his father disapproved because he was not yet a man and told him to destroy the lot. Richardson was happy to hear that Philip and Freddy were taking drawing lessons, and hoped Hayd would join them. The architect asked his son about the carrier pigeons and about his hunting and said he was delighted to hear that Hayd had bagged a partridge. He looked forward to getting back to Brookline, when the two of them might go gunning together. According to his probate inventory, Richardson owned a double-barrel breach-loading shotgun as well as a fishing rod, but it is doubtful that he often found the time or, by this period in his life, the agility to use them.

At the end of the letter to his son, Richardson ordered the meals he wanted on his return. For Saturday supper, when he hoped his assistants Alexander W. Longfellow and Charles A. Coolidge would join the family (perhaps so he could mediate a peace treaty between them), he would have four courses: "plain" oyster soup, lobster *en coquille*, roast duck, and mushrooms on toast. On Sunday, "as a matter of course," he looked forward to broiled partridges. Finally he signed off, "Your much tired but loving father."

In another fragment of a letter written during this extended journey, the architect complained about lack of correspondence from the children. "Tell Harry Phil, Fred & Mary they are all a set of ungrateful children not to write me." In a postscript he took Hayd into his confidence, joking with him about hiring a female private secretary. Richardson had decided to get one who could take shorthand, and asked his son to begin collecting ads from the newspapers. He wanted him to help find a "good looking sprightly young woman[;] widow & old maids need not apply[;] nothing over 25. N.B. Dont trust your mother's judgement!!"

In another letter to Hayd, sent from Brookline in late December 1885, the architect mixed private and professional concerns as he reminded his son, who was now himself in Chicago, to be "very polite" to Frances Glessner if he met her because "you know I am designing a house for her." Hayd had received an invitation to attend the famous Mikado Ball given by the Marshall Fields for their children on New Year's Day 1886. Gilbert and Sullivan's new operetta of the same name, set in the Japanese court, was then all the rage, and the Fields' party used

the show as its motif. Hayd did attend the event, with Father reassuring him that Ned—the dog, not the landlord—was not being neglected in his absence. He also sent advice: "Keep your bowels open, your teeth white & never forget that you are a guest. . . . Dont leave family letters lying around loose[;] servants are fond of prying. . . . Be polite & cordial even, if you choose, but familiar with no one. Dont laugh too loud or immoderately. Get all the sleep you can." (In a later letter Richardson advises, regarding regularity, that "if magnesia don't work try Hathorne water.") This seems to be a Victorian updating of the very similar advice on manners and morals contained in Lord Chesterfield's celebrated eighteenth-century letters to his son, a copy of which the architect had in his library. And finally there was a note on sightseeing: visit the stockyards and the "very fine" park system designed by Olmsted, the father advised his son, but "there is no public building in Chicago worth seeing." With this the architect disowned the American Express Company building he had designed for the city in 1872, before he had found his own brand of commercial architecture.

The series of late houses produced by Richardson represented architectural achievement of the highest order, but on a relatively small scale. Any architect worth his salt, especially one trained at the École des Beaux-Arts, aspired to create monumental buildings for government and commerce. Richardson was no exception. He told John Glessner that he would design anything from a cathedral to a chicken coop, for design was his business. Over the course of his career opportunities had arisen to create just such big works, but in his last years, in buildings like the Chamber of Commerce in Cincinnati, the Marshall Field Wholesale Store in Chicago's Loop, and, largest of all, the Allegheny County Courthouse and attached jail in Pittsburgh, he sealed his lasting fame. If Trinity formed the cornerstone of his career, these were the capstones.

Marshall Field himself was slightly older than Richardson. Born in rustic Conway in the foothills of the Berkshires in western Massachusetts, he headed West before the Civil War to seek and find his fortune. He had risen rapidly from a clerkship to head of the Chicago department store that still bears his name, and went on to build a vast fortune in urban real estate and other interests. Marshall

H. H. Richardson, Marshall Field Wholesale Store, Chicago, Illinois, 1885–87. The now-demolished building opened on the eve of the arrival of the steel-framed skyscraper.

Field & Company was established in 1881 with a retail division catering to the wants of modish women and a wholesale branch serving the needs of out-of-town traveling salesmen. In April 1885 Field asked Richardson to design a new wholesale building for a large half-block site on the western side of the Loop. He would personally own the building and lease it to the company.

As at Cincinnati, when the "famous architect" hit Chicago on a fact-finding tour in October 1885, the local press interviewed him in his rooms, at the Grand Pacific Hotel near the proposed site. The reporter for the *Tribune* learned from Richardson that "beauty will be one of the objects aimed at in the plans, but it will be a beauty of material and symmetry rather than of mere superficial ornamentation." Field's retail store might need ornament to attract the ladies, but the wholesale branch meant for the traveling man need sport no frills. Richardson said he had been studying the problem of the commercial facade for some time, and the Field Store "will be as plain as it can be made, the effects depending on the relations of the 'voids and solids'—that is, on the proportion of the parts." In confident words and seductive drawings the architect convinced the reporter that "the structure will be a distinct advance in the architecture of buildings devoted to commercial purposes in this country." Norcross Brothers built the store of Missouri pink granite, and it opened for business more than a year after the architect's death.

Richardson provided in this, one of his last works, a building "which in massiveness, simplicity of lines, and admirable blending of artistic beauty with adaptability to its purpose" appeared to the writer Charles Dudley Warner "unrivalled

Main stair, Allegheny County Courthouse, Pittsburgh, 1883–88. Only in Piranesi's Carceri *etchings do we otherwise find such genius in the manipulation of arcuated forms in diagonal spaces, and unlike Piranesi's, Richardson's conception was actually built.*

in this country." And to an up-and-coming Chicago architect named Louis Sullivan, the store rose as "a monument to trade, to the organized commercial spirit, to the power and progress of the age." At the beginning of the crest of his own career, Sullivan stood in awe of the building and its creator. On the exterior it was a simple horizontal ashlar block articulated by a series of arcades whose rhythm and scale varied as they rose. Both Richardson and Field had visited Florence in the years preceding the design of the store, so it should come as no surprise that the architect adapted the exterior from the great palazzi associated with Renaissance merchant princes such as the Medici. But the design also made reference to Field's origins and those of the dry goods he wholesaled from the building, for in its heavy-timber construction and its brick western wall, opened with row upon row of segmentally arched windows, the Field Store recalled the characteristic architecture of the New England textile mill. The architect had known classmates at Harvard, such as Benjamin Crowninshield, whose families owned such mills at Lowell, Massachusetts, and Concord, New Hampshire. In Chicago, Richardson managed to create a commercial block intended to celebrate distant and recent commercial and manufacturing history. Once again memory made up part of the mix.

Indeed, memory prevailed over technology in the Field facades as in all of Richardson's works. A drawing exists showing that the architect or his builders thought of using a structural iron box girder spanning above the first-floor windows. Whether or not this actually occurred is unknown and irrelevant. Important is the fact that, according to the drawing, this element of nineteenth-century engineering would have been completely buried within the stone-faced exterior. No matter what structural help the iron might have provided, the principal Field facades were to appear as traditional and massive load-bearing masonry walls. The architect sought to give his building meaning by association with the past, not the present.

Despite its conservative appearance, the proto-modernist Louis Sullivan recognized Richardson's Marshall Field Wholesale Store as an "oasis" or "landmark," one that showed "when and where architecture has taken on its outburst of form as a grand passion." Although unceremoniously demolished in 1930 to make way for a parking lot that still occupies the site, the store has always seemed to historians to have been architecturally one of the most important commercial blocks of the years just before the rise of the sky-scraper. It confronted the street with a scale, a monu-

Exterior detail, Allegheny County Jail, Pittsburgh, 1883–88. The low-sprung archway of huge identical voussoirs is a most characteristic Richardsonian form, one that reflects the architect's admiration for the French and Spanish Romanesque.

mental unity, that was new in the American city. Although quickly overtopped by the next generation—of steel-framed office buildings—its dignified presence continued to impress until the day of its destruction.

"If they honor me for the pygmy things I have already done," Richardson allegedly said near the end of his life, "what will they say when they see Pittsburgh finished?" He referred to the culminating monumental works of his truncated career, the courthouse and jail designed by him and erected by Norcross for Allegheny County, Pennsylvania, between 1883 and 1888. He won the commission in a limited competition with four other architects of local and national reputation. And he demanded and got a 5 percent commission when the county had expected to pay him 3 percent.

The courthouse is a public landmark embodying the "majesty of the law"; its civic stature called for a design rich in silhouette and ornamental embellishment. These characteristics had to be joined to practical considerations, however: ease of access, clarity of circulation, plenty of natural light and air. Richardson drew upon his Parisian training to lay out an arrangement of courtrooms off a corridor surrounding a central courtyard. Each of the courtrooms is lighted from both the outside and the courtyard. A heating and ventilation system, inspired by the House of Parliament in London, which Richardson inspected during his 1882 trip abroad, took in air through the circular "nostrils" at the top of the main tower, heated or cooled it in the basement, distributed it throughout the building, and then expelled it from the paired stair towers at the rear of the courtyard.

Inside and out, the architect enriched the courthouse with Romanesque columns, arches, and ornament, but the elemental architectural relationships of window and wall, the exterior ashlar masonry of alternating tiers of broad and narrow granite blocks set in red mortar, the play of arches in the entry and stair

Exterior detail, Allegheny County Courthouse, Pittsburgh, 1883–88. Romanesque details set into powerful granite walls: this is Richardson's reworking of the architecture he had studied in France and Spain during his lightning tour in 1882.

Exterior detail of the Allegheny County Courthouse, Pittsburgh, 1883–88. Robust arcuated forms, huge granite blocks, and subordinate ornamental accents create a memorable example of architecture as the embodiment of civic pride.

hall, and the exposed metallic framing of the courtrooms (an architectural expression of industrial material rare in Richardson's work, and not part of the building he knew before he died) are what make this one of the most impressive public buildings in America. Other architects often copied its design in the dozen or so years after its completion.

Behind the courthouse and connected to it by a "Bridge of Sighs" spanning an intervening street, the jail is a limited-access building in which the decorative parts of the courthouse are eliminated in favor of even more elemental architectural values. A high wall, administration wing, and L-shaped warden's residence enclose a traditional radial arrangement of cell blocks. The memorable public feature is the jailhouse wall, an almost windowless mass of layered ashlar stones set in red mortar and relieved by a midheight water table and a monumental archway. This arch springs from the ground as a half circle of eight-foot uncarved voussoirs of a kind Richardson had admired in Spain during his European trip, and it may be the single motif that expresses his aesthetic in its purest form. It radiates all the simplicity and power, all the quietude and massiveness, all the conservative stamp of memory that he could have wished.

Interior detail, Allegheny County Courthouse, Pittsburgh, 1883–88. The architect "signed" some of his buildings with various forms of his monogram.

As this array of grand buildings came off the drafting boards in Brookline, the architect's physical problems continued to mount. His indispositions kept pace with his expanding girth and during the last period of his life increasingly restricted his movements. "I know you have no carriage strong enough to carry me from the depot," he had written to Henry Adams—perhaps tongue in cheek, perhaps not—as early as July 1884. According to one client, Nicholas Anderson, with whom he stayed on one of his last visits to Washington, he had become a "great deal of trouble. He bullies and nags everybody; makes great demands upon our time and service; must ride, even if he has to go but a square; gets up at noon; and has to have his meals sent to his room." By early 1886 he was largely confined to the Cottage Street house in Brookline under the care of a Dr. Williams. He reported "living very quiet[ly] for me" in a letter to a traveling George Shepley at the beginning of the year and "feeling generally *very* well," although his hernia continued to bother him.

Early in 1886 Julia Richardson visited Washington with their oldest daughter, leaving the architect stuck in Brookline. From confinement he wrote letters to her at Wormley's Hotel that carried solicitations about her health and worries about his work under construction there, both personal and professional concerns characteristically flowing from his pen in one long continuous stream. "I was very sorry to hear that you were hoarse again. Wear two undershirts if the

Exterior detail, Allegheny County Courthouse, Pittsburgh, 1883–88. The parti-colored random ashlar of Richardson's early work gave way in his later buildings to a mono-chromatic layered stonework with alternating widths, but the sense of massive solidity remained.

weather is extreme," he wrote to his wife. "Dont fail to see the Anderson house. . . . Write me about the Hay house—the marble mantel in Hall—the dining room—the library. Tell Henry [Adams] I am making a wrought iron & plate glass screen for his study mantel."

The next day, February 7, he wrote again, surrounded by his children, the family dog, and the Irish help. He expressed delight in receiving letters from the travelers, but was as usual frustrated by their lack of news. "Why dont somebody write me about the Hay house & the Anderson house. I am longing to hear what you think of them. . . . As much as I want you & as much as I suppose you want to get back I beg you not to hurry that is if you feel you are improving & having a good time. Buy all you want & have a good time." This seemingly energetic jumble of prose might suggest a man full of vitality if we did not know otherwise. The letter also reports that he had had a "crisis" while Julia was away. He had suffered two "great abscesses" in his ear. Drs. Williams and Blake had come in for consultation, and he had been unable to host a dinner party on Saturday. "Little Mary," his fifteen-year-old daughter, "presided all alone." The pain continued, he admitted, but he thought he would be better by the next day, when the abscesses should burst. He had been unable to eat anything, unable to chew even moistened bread, had taken nothing but gruel and milk. In the face of all this his positive attitude was undampened, or perhaps his denial in full flower. He added that he felt otherwise "remarkably well," chatted about his various visitors, both friends and clients, and announced that, if he could chew the next day, he was going to ask the Glessners to join him for supper at the Country Club. He did not. When they arrived they found him confined to bed in the room at the top of the stairs, although "mentally as alert as usual."

Richardson wrote the second letter to his wife in Washington just over two months before he died, on April 27, 1886. In that last period he was surrounded by his two abiding concerns, work and family. During his last months, F. L. Olmsted wrote to Mariana Van Rensselaer, the architect had more to do than ever, and "never had such assurance of his leadership and the public's grateful acceptance of it." When Olmsted had last seen him, in Washington, he had seemed at first extremely weak and downcast, "hardly able to speak," but when the subject of architecture arose, for an hour "he discussed upon the works that he had in hand, upon his office, and upon his methods of work in his most animated, cheerful, sometimes even hilarious spirit, and so strongly and clearly" that Olmsted said he would report that he had never seen him in better condition. It was a final, misleading burst of energy.

Thereafter Richardson kept mainly to his bed, believing for a time that the

Exterior with Bridge of Sighs and warden's house, Allegheny County Jail, Pittsburgh, 1883–88. The stereometry of these forbidding granite ashlar jailhouse walls has only rarely been equalled in the history of architecture.

doctors would cure him and planning to go to Nantucket in preparation for another trip to Europe. But at some point he must finally have faced the gravity of his situation, for he told one physician that he wanted just two more years, "to see the Pittsburgh Court-house and the Chicago store complete." So he lingered in the bedroom at the top of the stairs, embraced by his family and framed by photographs and sketches of his work pinned to the cork-lined walls, until on April 27, 1886, again to quote Olmsted, "the sleep came in which he passed away so quietly and softly that no one present knew when death occurred." Phillips Brooks was to liken his departure from life to the "vanishing of a great mountain from the landscape." Given the character of some of Richardson's finest works, the geological metaphor was indeed apt.

Richardson's life during his last years was a mixture of artistic triumph and fatal illness. For no one else is that oft-quoted truism of the tenth-century monk

Notker of St. Gall more readily applicable than for him—in the midst of life he was certainly in death. For no one else is that haunting line from an Emily Dickinson letter of 1863 so apt: "Life is death we're lengthy at, death the hinge to life." For during his last decade Richardson was dying on his feet, although his innate optimism refused to recognize the fact. The documents swing between the architectural strengths exemplified by his buildings and the physical frailties belied by his apparent robustness. He died at the crest of his career. Death rarely happens "on time," but in the case of this architect, its coming was truly untimely.

❖   ❖   ❖

AFTER A SERVICE AT TRINITY CHURCH ON APRIL 30, THE ARCHITECT was buried at Walnut Hill Cemetery in Brookline. He left behind three interconnected legacies: his family, his firm, and his impact on American architecture. His reckless disregard for financial order in the short run left his family somewhat in the lurch. He died intestate and insolvent, his affairs in shambles—"in a condition," according to Olmsted, "showing his characteristic, unconquerable recklessness in personal matters." His gross income by the end of his life must have been large, "far larger than any other architect" then in practice, yet he lived in a rented house and he died deeply in debt. To the end he focused on his work to the exclusion of all else. He refused to accept that his hold on life was tenuous, refused to put his personal affairs in order, and so left his family—a forty-eight-year-old widow with six children still at home—almost nothing but bills. Julia, fortunately, had a small income of her own, and Ned Hooper charged her only nominal rent for the Perkins place until she was able to buy it, so no one in the family starved or was left homeless.

In the long run Richardson left behind a family that was to become significantly involved in his profession. Some dozen and a half of his direct and collateral descendants practiced and continue to practice architecture, while others have worked in the related fields of construction and landscape design. Although they have, of course, evolved their own styles in accordance with their own place and time, they extended his architectural reach into the fifth generation on the East and West Coasts and in New Orleans. Architecture, it might be said, continues to be the family business.

Richardson had included his children in the work of the studio—or at least they thought that he had—but his family and architecture first became officially intertwined when his daughter Jula married George Shepley, in June 1886, just two months after her father's death. The architect had welcomed his chief assistant and legman into the family in a letter written in March, a letter in which he gave the couple his permission to announce their engagement. And then, in an enigmatic and sad comment, Richardson introduced a hint of growing distance

OPPOSITE: *Exterior, Allegheny County Courthouse, Pittsburgh, 1883–88. The main tower took in air through the "nostrils" at the top of the turrets, air that was sent to the basement to be cleaned, warmed, or cooled, and distributed through the building via a system like that Richardson had studied at the Houses of Parliament in London.*

between himself and his daughter. A relationship that seems so uniformly loving in Julia Richardson Shepley's own reminiscence received a different interpretation from the architect: "I have not spoken to Jula," he wrote to Shepley. "I never have—about this—You know my regard for you—you may know some day what it is never to have had the entire love of a daughter except as a child." Perhaps as she grew older Jula began to resent the priorities of her father's life, in which work came first and all else followed. In any event the couple's marriage sealed the relationship between Richardson's family and Richardson's profession. Their first son, Henry Richardson Shepley, was born within the year in his grandfather's cork-lined bedroom at the top of the stairs. He too attended Harvard and the École, practiced architecture, and eventually became head of the firm of Shepley, Rutan and Coolidge.

That firm was born on the last day of Richardson's life. In handwriting that remained surprisingly steady, he penned an informal, unsigned will directing that his business be carried on by three trusted assistants, Charles H. Rutan, Charles A. Coolidge, and George F. Shepley. As Shepley, Rutan and Coolidge until 1915, the firm designed Stanford University, the Harvard Medical School in Boston, the Public Library and Art Institute in Chicago, and a host of other important buildings. As Shepley Bulfinch Richardson and Abbott, the firm still survives and—among countless other major works—recently completed the South Quadrangle Development for the Smithsonian Institution in Washington. Until just a few years ago a direct descendant of Richardson himself held the rank of a principal in the office.

Richardson's broadest and deepest legacy, however, was to American architecture in general, and it is here that his historical stature is defined. His influence ranged from the work of those architects who copied the Richardson Romanesque in buildings spread across the land in the last years of the nineteenth century to the monumental achievements of men such as Charles McKim, Stanford White, Langford Warren, and John Galen Howard, who did not follow his medievalizing style but pursued his devotion to architecture as high public art. Had he no other followers, his historical place would be assured, but his work also inspired another group of men, midwesterners led by Louis H. Sullivan and Frank Lloyd Wright, who continued his development of an American architecture and raised it to world-class importance.

Sullivan and Wright saw Richardson's work against the backdrop of his time. His was an eclectic period in which American architecture was dominated by European historical styles. He alone in his day sought to reinterpret the architecture of the medieval past in the light of emerging American urbanism on the one hand and the robustness of the American landscape on the other. Whereas Richard Morris Hunt and other of his contemporaries wanted to transfer European styles to America, Richardson sought to adapt the weight and measure of the Romanesque to the commercial forms that had appeared in some American cities in the middle of the nineteenth century and to American geological forms when he was designing for the suburbs or countryside. Hunt and others wanted to rival Europe by appropriating its accomplishments; Richardson wanted to create an architecture rooted in the old forms but adapted to a new situation. The sturdiness of his results overpowered the brittleness of his contemporaries' works just as it continues to overpower the lightweight forms of much subsequent building.

But Richardson's achievement does not rest on his historical position alone. His attention to the elements of architecture produced buildings that are, ultimately, ahistorically superb. His control of form, quiet but animated by a play of symmetry and asymmetry, by the sparkle of natural materials, by the studied relationship of part to part, window to wall, roof to mass, inside to outside, space to space; his creation of buildings that continue to radiate authority through their sheer presence, their weight, measure, and grounded proportions—these characteristics still engage the observer. As does Richardson's versatility: his works range from the glacial forms of the Ames gate lodge and the Paine house to the urbane elegance of the Hay and Adams houses and the rugged individualism of the Glessner house. Not all of his works reach the highest level of achievement, but those houses, his libraries and railroad depots, Trinity Church, the Marshall Field Wholesale Store, and the Pittsburgh courthouse and jail all rank high in American—even world—cultural achievement.

And finally, Richardson's career proves that architecture of lasting quality and historical importance can be achieved by a conservative approach, by generating buildings that transfer the richness of past accomplishment rather than embrace a paucity of present choices. Twentieth-century historians championed those modern architects whose work seemed progressive, while belittling those whose works they could deride as traditional. But Richardson turned away from the technology of his time to find inspiration in preindustrial architecture. He did this not to ape the past, as did so many of his contemporaries, or to merge it with new technology, as did others, but to find a tradition of excellence that he could continue to develop by matching it to the society of his own time and place. The measure of his success is demonstrated by the important position many of his buildings still hold in American cultural history.

NOTES

1. CINCINNATI: 1885

9 *"A mournful object for size"*: Nicholas Anderson to his son, 31 January 1883, *Larz Anderson, Letters and Journals of a Diplomat*, ed. by Isabel Anderson (New York: Fleming H. Revell Company, 1940), 207; Cass Gilbert to DeLisle Stewart, 26 January 1914 (Gilbert Papers, Library of Congress); Marc Friedlaender, "Henry Hobson Richardson, Henry Adams, and John Hay," *Journal of the Society of Architectural Historians* 29 (October 1970): 238.

10 *ten best buildings*: "The Ten Best Buildings in the United States," *The American Architect and Building News* 17 (13 June 1885): 282.

10 *"They have made much of me"*: H. H. Richardson (hereafter HHR) to Julia Richardson, 27 January 1885 (Department of Printing and Graphic Arts, Houghton Library, Harvard University).

11 *A reporter*: "A Distinguished Architect," *Commercial Gazette*, 27 January 1885, 8.

11 *This writer resorted*: "The New 'Change,'" *Cincinnati Enquirer*, 9 June 1885, 4.

12 *In December 1884*: *Dedicatory Exercises at the Opening of the New Building of the Cincinnati Chamber of Commerce* (Cincinnati, 1889); *Richardson, the Architect, and the Cincinnati Chamber of Commerce Building* (Cincinnati: The Cincinnati Astronomical Society, 1914); J. William Rudd, "The Cincinnati Chamber of Commerce Building," *Journal of the Society of Architectural Historians* 27 (May 1968): 115–23.

12 *The chamber's administrative officer*: Biographical descriptions of the members of the Chamber of Commerce are drawn from Charles Theodore Greve, *Centennial History of Cincinnati and Representative Citizens* (Chicago: Biographical Publishing Company, 1904), and other biographical dictionaries.

13 *"'I am my own music'"*: *The Letters of Mrs. Henry Adams, 1865–1883*, ed. Ward Thoron (Boston: Little, Brown & Company, 1936), 7 May 1882.

14 *Richardson reveled*: Given the present fascination with sexual orientation in biographical writing, it should be noted that this seems to have been merely social and professional preference. There is no hint of homoeroticism in the record.

14 *"Cincinnati ware"*: Registry of Probate, Norfolk County Court house, Dedham, Massachusetts (H. H. Richardson [1886] #24978, document 9).

16 *In one the group stands*: For this photograph see James F. O'Gorman, *Henry Hobson Richardson and His Office: Selected Drawings* (Cambridge, Mass.: Harvard University Library, 1974), 17.

16 *"the equator of the waistcoat"*: Frederick Squires, *Architectonics: Tales of Tom Thumtack* (New York: William T. Comstock Co., 1914).

16 *The English author*: Osbert Sitwell, *Left Hand, Right Hand!* (Boston: Little, Brown & Company, 1944).

16 *One client complained*: "Mourned by Lovers of Art," *New York Star*, 2 May 1886, 2.

16 *At just this moment*: M. Friedlaender, "Henry Hobson Richardson, Henry Adams, and John Hay."

16 *One obituary remembered*: "Mourned by Lovers of Art."

17 *His daughter Julia*: Mrs. George F. Shepley, "Reminiscences" (unpublished typescript at the Department of Printing and Graphic Arts, Houghton Library, Harvard University).

17 *His friend and professional colleague*: Peter B. Wight, obituary of H. H. Richardson, *Inland Architect* 7 (May 1886): 59–61.

17 *One of Richardson's chief assistants*: Charles A. Coolidge, "Henry Hobson Richardson," in *Later Years of the Saturday Club*, ed. M. A. De Wolfe Howe (Boston and New York: Houghton Mifflin Company, 1927), 193–200.

17 *They printed memoirs*: [A. G. Clark], *A Bull-Doggerel, Entitled A Bouquet of Loose Flowers*, Hengstenberg Lunch Table Fifth Anniversary [Cincinnati, 1885]; C. Coolidge, "Richardson."

18 *This displayed hearty camaraderie*: A copy of this document is among the Richardson papers at the Department of Printing and Graphic Arts, Houghton Library, Harvard University. The loving cup itself seems lost.

18 *They may not have known*: Royal Cortissoz, *Art and Common Sense* (New York: C. Scribner's Sons, 1913), 384.

18 *Richardson was laid up*: HHR to Henry Adams, 7 June 1885 (Massachusetts Historical Society).

19 *The chamber occupied*: "Cincinnati Chamber of Commerce," *Building: An Architectural Monthly* 3 (August 1885): 126.

21 *Although few architectural critics*: Charles Dudley Warner, *Studies in the South and West* (New York: Harper & Brothers, 1889), 267–68. The building was destroyed by fire in 1914. In recent years some of its stonework was incorporated in a monument to the architect across from the university.

2. NEW ORLEANS: 1838–55

23 *A combination of Southern grace*: C. Coolidge, "Richardson."

23 *We know he bragged*: Phillips Brooks, *Essays and Addresses* (New York: E. P. Dutton and Co., 1894), 482 ff.; "Some Incidents in the Life of H. H. Richardson," *The American Architect and Building News* 20 (23 October 1886): 198–99; James F. O'Gorman, "On Vacation with H. H. Richardson," *Archives of American Art Journal* 19 (1979): 2–14.

23 *That did not become generally*: F. W. Gibbs, *Joseph Priestley* (London: T. Nelson, 1965); Caroline Robbins, "'Honest Heretic': Joseph Priestley in America, 1774–1804," *Proceedings of the American Philosophical Society* 106 (1962): 60 ff.

24 *A cartoon by James Sayers*: James F. O'Gorman, *H. H. Richardson: Architectural Forms for an American Society* (Chicago: University of Chicago Press, 1987), 4.

27 *By the time of the congressional ratification:* Information about the Priestley, Richardson, and Bein families is drawn largely from a variety of published and unpublished sources, among them Lillian C. Bourgeois, *Cabanocey: The History, Customs and Folklore of St. James Parish* (New Orleans; Pelican Publishing Company, 1957); the records of St. James Parish (kindly abstracted for me by Mrs. Marie Campbell of Vacherie, Louisiana); the Gibson, Cohen, and other directories of New Orleans; and the notarial records (especially those of D. L. McCay) of the city.

27 *It was a fair day:* Valcour Aime, *Plantation Diary of the Late Mr. Valcour Aime* (New Orleans: Clark and Hofeline, 1878).

28 *The economy of antebellum:* T. B. Thorpe, "Sugar and Sugar Regions of Louisiana," *Harper's Monthly* 7 (1853): 746–67; Charles P. Roland, *Louisiana Sugar Plantations During the American Civil War* (Leiden: E. J. Brill, 1957).

30 *The plantation is the subject:* Eliza Ripley, *Social Life in Old New Orleans* (New York and London: D. Appleton and Company, 1912), chap. 25.

31 *Priestley Plantation lacked:* An inventory of the plantation was taken a year after the death, in 1857, of Margaret Fulker Priestley. It is filed under her name in the Succession Records at the New Orleans Public Library.

33 *The combination of:* Robert C. Reinders, *End of a Era: New Orleans, 1850–1860* (New Orleans: Pelican Publishing Company, 1964).

33 *While the antebellum period:* Theodore Clapp, *Autobiographical Sketches and Recollections During a Thirty-five Years' Residence in New Orleans*, 2d ed. (Boston: Phillips, Sampson & Co., 1858), 185.

34 *The Anglophile Julia Street row:* Samuel Wilson Jr. et al., eds., *New Orleans Architecture*, volume 2, *The American Sector* (Gretna, La.: Pelican Publishing Company, 1972), 174–77.

35 *Eliza Ripley also:* Ripley, *Social Life*, chap. 23.

35 *Parson Clapp's church:* John F. C. Waldo, *Historical Sketch of the First Unitarian Church of New Orleans, La.* (New Orleans: The Church, 1907).

35 *It witnessed much:* Henry Didimus, *New Orleans As I Found It* (New York: Harper and Brothers, 1845).

37 *The firm of Priestley:* The firm's itemized advertisements appear often in city directories during this period.

37 *After the Civil War:* See the family tree given in the Julia Shepley Papers in the Archives of American Art.

37 *This generated letters:* John Coolidge, "H. H. Richardson's Youth: Some Unpublished Documents," in *In Search of Modern Architecture: A Tribute to Henry-Russell Hitchcock*, ed. Helen Searing (Cambridge, Mass., and London: M.I.T. Press, 1982), 165–71.

38 *To the information:* Mariana Griswold Van Rensselaer, *Henry Hobson Richardson and His Works* (Boston: Houghton, Mifflin Company, 1888), chap. 1.

3. CAMBRIDGE: 1855–59

41 *The Harvard College class:* William Braverman, "James Benjamin Clark and the Southern Experience at Harvard College in the Civil War Era," *Harvard Library Bulletin* 34 (Fall 1986): 396–414.

41 *For the most part:* Henry Adams, *The Education of Henry Adams: An Autobiography* (Boston: Houghton Mifflin Company, 1918).

41 *The nearly daily entries:* Benjamin W. Crowninshield, *A Private Journal, 1856–1858* (Cambridge, Mass.: privately printed, 1941).

41 *Harvard when Richardson:* Bainbridge Bunting and Margaret Henderson Floyd, *Harvard: An Architectural History* (Cambridge, Mass., and London: Harvard University Press, 1985).

43 *He bought a copy:* Ticknor and Company Ledgers, fMS 1185.14[3], f. 669 (Houghton Library, Harvard University); John Coolidge, "Richardson's Youth," in *In Search of Modern Architecture*, ed. Helen Searing (Cambridge, Mass.: M.I.T. Press, 1982).

43 *Adams's biographer Ernest Samuels:* Ernest Samuels, *The Young Henry Adams* (Cambridge, Mass.: Harvard University Press, 1948).

44 *The venerable old college:* Samuel Eliot Morison, *Three Centuries of Harvard* (Cambridge, Mass.: Harvard University Press, 1936).

44 *While he borrowed no books:* Harvard College Library Charging List, 1855–59 (Harvard University Archives).

46 *Like many another Southerner:* Phillips Brooks, *Essays and Addresses* (New York: E. P. Dutton and Co., 1894).

48 *The foundations of the Porcellian:* A. T. Perkins, "The Porcellian Club," *The Harvard Book* (Cambridge, Mass., 1875), vol. 2, 349.

49 *We know most about:* J. Coolidge, "Richardson's Youth."

51 *In June 1856:* Records of the College Faculty XV, 1855–1860 (Harvard University Archives), 55.

52 *His undergraduate nickname:* J. O'Gorman, *H. H. Richardson*, 9.

53 *To hold the water:* O'Gorman, *H. H. Richardson*, 83.

54 *At the beginning of Richardson's:* J. Coolidge, "Richardson's Youth."

4. PARIS: 1859–65

57 *By mid-September:* Van Rensselaer, *Richardson*, chap. 2.

57 *Between 1852 and 1870:* David Pinkney, *Napoleon III and the Rebuilding of Paris* (Princeton: Princeton University Press, 1958); David Van Zanten, *Building Paris* (New York: Cambridge University Press, 1994).

57 *Not all observers: Pages from the Concourt Journal*, ed., trans. Robert Baldick (London and New York: Oxford University Press, 1962).

58 *Later, in 1883:* Sue A. Kohler and Jeffrey R. Carson, *Sixteenth Street Architecture* (Washington, D.C.: Commission of Fine Arts, 1978), 159.

59 *Once ensconced as a member:* Richard Chafee, "Richardson's Record at the Ecole des Beaux-Arts," *Journal of the Society of Architectural Historians* 36 (October 1977): 175–88.

59 *By Richardson's time:* David Van Zanten, *Designing Paris* (Cambridge, Mass.: M.I.T. Press, 1987).

60 *Once admitted as a student:* Richard Chafee, "The Teaching of Architecture at the Ecole des Beaux-Arts," in *The Architecture of the Ecole des Beaux-Arts*, ed. Arthur Drexler (New York: Museum of Modern Art, 1977), 61–109.

61 *Hunt soon became:* Paul Baker, *Richard Morris Hunt* (Cambridge, Mass.: M.I.T. Press, 1980).

61 *James Freret also stemmed:* Edwin L. Jewell's *Crescent City Illustrated* (New Orleans: E. L. Jewell, 1873), 127.

61 *His later drawings:* A collection of Freret's drawings and some biographical information are in the Southeastern Architectural Archives at Tulane University, New Orleans.

63 *There he found himself:* Henry Adams, *Correspondence,* ed. by J. C. Levenson (Cambridge, Mass.: Harvard University Press, 1982).

63 *He reached Paris:* Van Rensselaer, *Richardson.*

64 *He rose to the rank:* Andrew B. Booth, *Records of Louisiana Confederate Soldiers and Louisiana Confederate Commands* (New Orleans: Commissioner of Military Records, 1920); John McGrath, "In a Louisiana Regiment," *Southern Historical Society Papers* 31 (January-December 1903): 103–20.

64 *In a letter written:* J. Coolidge, "Richardson's Youth," in *In Search of Modern Architecture,* ed. Helen Searing (Cambridge, Mass.: M.I.T. Press, 1982).

64 *As early as mid-August 1861:* Julia Shepley Papers, Archives of American Art.

65 *Even during his bolt:* Chafee, "Richardson's Record."

67 *On June 3, 1863:* Van Rensselaer, *Richardson,* 142.

68 *André in particular:* T. M. Clark, letter to the editor, *The Nation* 47 (1888): 151.

68 *Richardson studied:* Van Zanten, *Designing Paris.*

69 *He seemed:* Peter B. Wight, obituary.

71 *One version of the story:* T. M. Clark, *The Nation:* 47:151.

71 *According to another version:* P. B. Wight, obituary.

71 *As a member:* Pierre-Marie Auzas, *Eugene Viollet le Duc 1814–1879* ([Paris]: Caisse Nationale des Monuments Historiques, 1979), 140.

72 *In Paris Richardson:* James F. O'Gorman, "An 1886 Inventory of H. H. Richardson's Library," *Journal of the Society of Architectural Historians* 41 (May 1982): 150–55.

5. NEW YORK: 1865–74

75 *Phillips Brooks emphasized:* Phillips Brooks, *Essays and Addresses* (New York: E. P. Dutton and Co., 1894).

76 *One of his fellow boarders:* "Some Incidents in the Life of H. H. Richardson," *American Architect and Building News* 20 (October 23, 1886): 198–99.

77 *His cousin:* Elizabeth Stevenson, *Park Maker: A Life of Frederick Law Olmsted* (New York: Macmillan, 1977).

77 *Indeed, Richardson's shopping:* Richard Chafee, "Richardson's Record at the Ecole des Beaux-Arts," *Journal of the Society of Architectural Historians* 36 (October 1977): 175–88.

77 *When Richardson split:* HHR to "Billy," 25 April 1866 (Department of Printing and Graphic Arts, Houghton Library, Harvard University).

78 *Through his urging:* For details of the commissioning of all of Richardson's buildings, see Jeffrey Ochsner, *H. H. Richardson: Complete Architectural Works,* new ed. (Cambridge, Mass.: M.I.T. Press, 1984).

79 *In April Julia wrote:* Julia Shepley Papers, Archives of American Art.

81 *According to his biographer:* American Architect and Building News 23 (7 January 1888): 4.

81 *At the time:* Elizabeth Barlow Rogers, *Frederick Law Olmsted's New York* (New York: Praeger, 1972).

82 *In a letter written:* Olmsted to [W. B.] Duncan, 22 September 1870 (Olmsted Papers, Library of Congress).

82 *The committee report:* Staten Island Improvement Commission, *Report of a Preliminary Scheme of Improvements* (New York, 1871).

83 *While he was working:* Julia Shepley Papers, Archives of American Art.

85 *In a letter to the architect:* Charles Learoyd to HHR, 21 March 1867 (Department of Printing and Graphic Arts, Houghton Library, Harvard University).

85 *High praise:* A drawing of William A. Potter's design for Grace Church is in the collection of the Society for the Preservation of New England Antiquities.

86 *The Dorsheimer house:* Francis R. Kowsky, "The William Dorsheimer house," *Art Bulletin* 62 (March 1980): 134–47.

87 *From Washington Richardson wrote:* HHR to Olmsted, 20 January 1885 (Olmsted Papers, Library of Congress).

92 *Charles Follen McKim and Stanford White:* Paul R. Baker, *Stanny: The Gilded Life of Stanford White* (New York: Free Press, 1989).

92 *In 1868 Richard Codman:* Richard Codman, *Reminiscences* (Boston: North Bennett Street Industrial School, 1923), 29–31.

94 *Between 1869 and 1876:* O'Gorman, *Selected Drawings,* 213.

6. TRINITY CHURCH: 1872–77

99 *By late 1871:* A. H. Chester, *Trinity Church in the City of Boston* (Cambridge, Mass.: J. Wilson and Son, 1888).

99 *On March 12, 1872:* O'Gorman, *Selected Drawings,* 42–43.

100 *"No obtrusive columns":* Consecration Services of Trinity Church, Boston (Boston, 1877).

100 *One of his friends:* "Mourned by Lovers of Art," *New York Star,* 2 May 1886.

101 *He made a distinction:* O'Gorman, *Selected Drawings,* 211.

101 *The day he heard:* Ann J. Adams, "The Birth of a Style: Henry Hobson Richardson and the Competition Drawings for Trinity Church, Boston," *Art Bulletin* 62 (September 1980): 409–33.

102 *References to sickness:* The draft report is in Trinity Church Archives.

102 *In an undated note:* HHR to Charles H. Parker (Trinity Church Archives).

102 *Richardson drew:* Theodore Stebbins Jr., "Richardson and Trinity Church: The Evolution of a Building," *Journal of the Society of Architectural Historians* 27 (December 1968): 281–98.

102 *Although the letter:* C. R. Codman to [George M.] Dexter, 31 May 1872 (Trinity Church Archives).

103 *According to White's letters:* Paul R. Baker, *Stanny: The Gilded Life of Stanford White* (New York: Free Press, 1989).

104 *According to one authority:* James F. O'Gorman, "O. W. Norcross: Richardson's 'Master Builder,'" *Journal of the Society of Architectural Historians* 32 (May 1973): 104–13.

104 *A veteran:* Mary Alice Molloy, "Richardson's Web: A Client's Assessment of the Architect's Home and Studio," *Journal of the Society of Architectural Historians* 54 (March 1995): 8–23.

104 *In the process:* O'Gorman, "O. W. Norcross."

104 *"Architects," he wrote:* O'Gorman, *Selected Drawings,* 212.

105 *They were working:* HHR to Phillips Brooks, 24 August 1874 (Richardson Papers, Archives of American Art).

105 *At the time of:* Consecration Services.

109 *But we are reminded: The Complete Poems of Emily Dickinson,* ed. Thomas H. Johnson (Boston: Little, Brown and Company, 1960), No. 451.

110 *Good work:* "Mourned by Lovers of Art."

111 *Almost every major:* Paul Clifford Larson and Susan M. Brown, eds., *The Spirit of H. H. Richardson on the Midland Prairies* (Ames, Iowa: Iowa State University Press, 1988).

7. BROOKLINE: 1874–82

113 *In the spring:* O'Gorman, *Selected Drawings,* 2–13.

113 *We know his assistants:* C. Coolidge, "Richardson"; Welles Bosworth, "I Knew H. H. Richardson," *Journal of the American Institute of Architects* 16 (September 1961):115–27.

114 *One draftsman remembered:* A. O. Elzner, "A Reminiscence of Richardson," *Inland Architect and News Record* 20 (September 1892): 15; see also E. P. Overmire, "A Draftsman's Recollection of Boston," *The Western Architect* 3 (February 1904): 18–20.

115 *As the architect's oldest child:* Julia Shepley, "Reminiscences" (Houghton Library, Harvard University).

116 *The sculptor Augustus Saint-Gaudens:* A. Saint-Gaudens, *Reminiscences,* ed. Homer Saint-Gaudens (New York: Century Co., 1913), vol. 1, 328–29.

116 *In a letter to Olmsted:* HHR to Olmsted, 23 August 1876 (Department of Printing and Graphic Arts, Houghton Library, Harvard University).

117 *Three years later:* Olmsted to Charles Eliot Norton, 9 November 1879 (Olmsted Papers, Library of Congress).

117 *Above the matchboard:* Mary Alice Molloy, "Richardson's Web: A Client's Assessment of the Architect's Home and Studio," *Journal of the Society of Architectural Historians* 54 (March 1995): 8–23.

118 *White doted on:* Paul R. Baker, *Stanny: The Gilded Life of Stanford White* (New York: Free Press, 1989).

118 *A room some twenty-five by thirty:* Elzner, "A Reminiscence."

119 *There they found:* Bosworth, "Richardson."

120 *He suggested to Olmsted:* O'Gorman, *Selected Drawings,* 122–24.

126 *Clover Adams: The Letters of Mrs. Henry Adams, 1865–1883,* ed. Ward Thoron (Boston: Little, Brown & Company, 1936), 22 April 1883.

126 *"His pleasure":* Larz Anderson, *Letters and Journals of a Diplomat,* ed. Isabel Anderson (New York: Fleming H. Revell Company, 1940), 5 November 1882.

126 *"It requires a severe":* Larz Anderson, *Letters,* 18 October 1882.

128 *The cause for this:* Letter quoted by permission of Susan and Stephen Paine, Cambridge, Massachusetts.

129 *The first Oliver Ames:* Robert F. Brown, "The Aesthetic Transformation of an Industrial Community," *Winterthur Portfolio* 12 (1977): 35–64.

131 *The nineteenth century created:* Leo Marx, *The Machine in the Garden* (New York: Oxford University Press, 1964).

132 *If the depot:* Ralph Waldo Emerson, "Nature" (1844), *Essays of Ralph Waldo Emerson* (New York: Thomas Y. Crowell Company, 1951), 382.

132 *It is, to appropriate: The Complete Poems of Emily Dickinson,* ed. Thomas H. Johnson (Boston: Little, Brown and Company, 1960), No. 712.

8. EUROPE: 1882

135 *In the summer of 1875:* Van Rensselaer, *Richardson.*

136 *They collectively weighed:* James F. O'Gorman, "On Vacation with H. H. Richardson: Ten Letters from Europe, 1882," *Archives of American Art Journal* 19 (1979): 20–29.

136 *Anecdotes of their progress:* "Three Notable Exceptions," *New York Tribune Sunday Magazine* 4 February 1912; "Too Good Not to Tell," *Old Farmers' Almanac* (1912), 51; Julia Shepley, "Reminiscences" (Houghton Library, Harvard University).

137 *In one, much to:* James Russell Lowell to Doña Emilia Gayangos de Riano in Madrid, 3 July 1882 (Department of Printing and Graphic Arts, Houghton Library, Harvard University).

137 *According to Herbert Jacques:* Van Rensselaer, *Richardson.*

137 *When George Shepley:* George Shepley in Paris to HHR, 30 July 1883, courtesy of Hugh Shepley.

139 *Richardson must have arranged:* Norman Kelvin, *The Collected Letters of William Morris* (Princeton: Princeton University Press, 1987), vol. 2, 113–14, 123–24.

139 *This, plus dropsy:* Charles W. Purdy, *Bright's Disease* (Philadelphia: Lea Brothers, 1886).

141 *"Architecture must be":* Phillips Brooks, *Letters of Travel* (New York: E. P. Dutton and Company, 1893); Alexander V. G. Allen, *Phillips Brooks, 1835–1893* (New York: E. P. Dutton, 1907), vol. 2, 460 ff.

149 *A passion hardly sated:* Shepley to HHR, 30 July 1883, courtesy of Hugh Shepley.

9. STUDIO DAYS: 1880s

153 *For the definitive image:* HHR to George Shepley, 31 December 1885 (Department of Printing and Graphic Arts, Houghton Library, Harvard University).

153 *Herkomer later wrote:* Richardson Papers, Archives of American Art.

153 *Herkomer presents:* John Hay to Julia Richardson, 29 April 1886 (John Hay Library, Brown University); Phillips Brooks, *Essays and Addresses* (New York: E. P. Dutton and Co., 1894).

153 *Whereas one observer:* A. O. Elzner, "A Reminiscence of Richardson," *Inland Architect and News Record* 20 (September 1892).

154 *"Mumps is mumps!":* HHR to Henry Adams, 18 July 1884 (Massachusetts Historical Society).

154 *"I have had a slight accident":* HHR to John Hay, 31 December 1885 (John Hay Library, Brown University).

155 *On one such Sunday:* O'Gorman, *Selected Drawings*, 2.

155 *Some months after:* HHR to Henry Lee Higginson, 6 November 1884 (Higginson Correspondence, Baker Library, School of Business, Harvard University).

156 *On a similar afternoon:* John B. Gass, "American Architecture and Architects," *Journal of the Royal Institute of British Architects*, n.s. 3 (6 February 1896): 232.

157 *One of them:* Welles Bosworth, "I Knew H. H. Richardson," *Journal of the American Institute of Architects* 16 (September 1961): 115–27.

157 *One observer called:* John B. Gass, "Some American Methods," in the Royal Institute of British Architects *Journal of Proceedings* n.s. 2 (18 March 1886): 179–88.

158 *Henry Irving:* Royal Institute of British Architects, *Journal of Proceedings* n.s. 2 (1885–86): 259.

158 *One one memorable occasion:* Elzner, "Reminiscence of Richardson."

159 *As the only École-trained:* Margaret Henderson Floyd, *Architecture After Richardson* (Chicago and London: University of Chicago Press, 1994), 44–59.

159 *In March 1886:* HHR to George Shepley, 14 March 1886 (Department of Printing and Graphic Arts, Houghton Library, Harvard University).

160 *Many years later:* Floyd, *Architecture After Richardson*, 44.

161 *For windows and other openings:* O'Gorman, *Selected Drawings*, 52–53.

162 *In 1881 Frederick Billings:* Richard H. Janson, "Mr. Billings' Richardson Library," *University of Vermont Alumni Magazine*, May 1963, 8–10.

164 *This self-assured document:* Van Rensselaer, *Richardson*, 147.

165 *He referred to an error:* O'Gorman, *Selected Drawings*, 171–74.

10. LAST WORKS: 1882–86

167 *"The youth gets":* The Journal of Henry David Thoreau, ed. Bradford Torrey and Francis H. Allen (Boston: Houghton Mifflin Company, 1906), vol. 4, 227.

168 *His study of French architecture:* Marc Friedlaender, "Henry Hobson Richardson, Henry Adams, and John Hay," *Journal of the Society of Architectural Historians* 29 (October 1970): 231–46.

170 *Erected on a site:* James F. O'Gorman, "A Tragic Circle," *Nineteenth Century* 2 (Autumn 1976): 46–49.

173 *Small, wiry, a teetotaler:* Mary Alice Molloy, "Richardson's Web: A Client's Assessment of the Architect's Home and Studio," *Journal of the Society of Architectural Historians* 54 (March 1995): 8–23.

177 *These contain:* HHR to Hayden [29 October and 28 December 1885] (Department of Printing and Graphic Arts, Houghton Library, Harvard University).

179 *As at Cincinnati:* James F. O'Gorman, "The Marshall Field Wholesale Store," *Journal of the Society of Architectural Historians* 37 (October 1978): 175–94.

179 *Richardson provided:* Charles Dudley Warner, *Studies in the South and West* (New York: Harper & Brothers, 1889).

180 *And to an up-and-coming:* Louis H. Sullivan, *Kindergarten Chats and Other Writings* (New York: George Wittenborn, Inc., 1947), 28–31.

181 *He won the commission:* "Mourned by Lovers of Art," *New York Star*, 2 May 1886.

181 *The courthouse is a public:* James D. Van Trump, *Majesty of the Law* (Pittsburgh: Pittsburgh History & Landmarks Foundation, 1988).

183 *According to one client:* Larz Anderson, *Letters and Journals of a Diplomat*, ed. Isabel Anderson (New York: Fleming H. Revell Co., 1940).

183 *He reported:* HHR to George Shepley, 2 January 1886 (Department of Printing and Graphic Arts, Houghton Library, Harvard University).

183 *From confinement:* HHR to Julia, 6–7 February 1886 (Department of Printing and Graphic Arts, Houghton Library, Harvard University).

184 *During his last months:* Olmsted to Mariana Van Rensselaer, 2 May 1886 (Olmsted Papers, Library of Congress).

187 *For no one else: The Letters of Emily Dickinson,* ed. Thomas H. Johnson (Cambridge, Mass.: Harvard University Press, 1958), vol. 2, 425.

187 *The architect had welcomed:* HHR to George Shepley, 14 March 1886 (Department of Printing and Graphic Arts, Houghton Library, Harvard University).

188 *In handwriting:* Department of Printing and Graphic Arts, Houghton Library, Harvard University.

188 *Had he no other followers:* James F. O'Gorman, *Three American Architects: Richardson, Sullivan, and Wright, 1865–1915* (Chicago: University of Chicago Press, 1991).

SELECTED READING

GENERAL:

Coolidge, Charles A. "Henry Hobson Richardson." In *Later Years of the Saturday Club*, edited by M. A. DeWolfe Howe. Boston and New York: Houghton Mifflin Company, 1927.

Floyd, Margaret Henderson. *Architecture After Richardson*. Chicago and London: University of Chicago Press, 1994.

Hitchcock, Henry-Russell. *The Architecture of H. H. Richardson and His Times*. New York: Museum of Modern Art, 1936 (and reprint).

Larson, Paul Clifford, and Susan M. Brown, eds. *The Spirit of H. H. Richardson on the Midland Prairies*. Ames, Iowa: Iowa State University Press, 1988.

Ochsner, Jeffrey Karl. *H. H. Richardson: Complete Architectural Works*. New ed. Cambridge, Mass.: M.I.T. Press, 1984.

O'Gorman, James F. *H. H. Richardson: Architectural Forms for an American Society*. Chicago and London: University of Chicago Press, 1987.

————. *Henry Hobson Richardson and His Office: Selected Drawings*. Cambridge, Mass.: Harvard University Library, 1974.

————. *Three American Architects: Richardson, Sullivan, and Wright, 1865–1915*. Chicago and London: University of Chicago Press, 1991.

Scully, Vincent J., Jr. *The Shingle Style: Architectural Theory and Design from Richardson to the Origins of Wright*. Rev. ed. New Haven: Yale University Press, 1974.

Van Rensselaer, Mariana Griswold. *Henry Hobson Richardson and His Works*. Boston: Houghton, Mifflin, 1888 (and reprints).

Wight, Peter B. "Obituary." *The Inland Architect and News Record* 7 (May 1886): 59–61.

1. CINCINNATI: 1885

Richardson, the Architect, and the Cincinnati Chamber of Commerce Building. Cincinnati: The Cincinnati Astronomical Society, 1914.

Rudd, J. William. "The Cincinnati Chamber of Commerce Building." *Journal of the Society of Architectural Historians* 27 (May 1968): 115–23.

2. NEW ORLEANS: 1838–55

Clapp, Theodore. *Autobiographical Sketches and Recollections During a Thirty-five Years' Residence in New Orleans*. 2d. ed. Boston: Phillips, Sampson & Co., 1858.

Ripley, Eliza. *Social Life in Old New Orleans*. New York and London: D. Appleton and Company, 1912.

Waldo, John F. C. *Historical Sketch of the First Unitarian Church of New Orleans, La*. New Orleans: The Church, 1907.

3. CAMBRIDGE: 1855–59

Adams, Henry. *The Education of Henry Adams: An Autobiography*. Boston: Houghton Mifflin Co., 1918 (and reprints).

Coolidge, John. "H. H. Richardson's Youth: Some Unpublished Documents." In *In Search of Modern Architecture: A Tribute to Henry-Russell Hitchcock*, edited by Helen Searing. Cambridge, Mass.: M.I.T. Press, 1982.

Crowninshield, Benjamin W. *A Private Journal, 1856–1858*. Cambridge, Mass.: Privately Printed, 1941.

4. PARIS: 1859–65

Chafee, Richard. "Richardson's Record at the Ecole des Beaux-Arts." *Journal of the Society of Architectural Historians* 36 (October 1977): 175–88.

Chafee, Richard. "The Teaching of Architecture at the Ecole des Beaux-Arts." In *The Architecture of the Ecole des Beaux-Arts*, edited by Arthur Drexler. New York: Museum of Modern Art, 1977.

5. NEW YORK: 1865–74

"Some Incidents in the Life of H. H. Richardson." *The American Architect and Building News* 20 (October 23, 1886): 198–299.

6. TRINITY CHURCH: 1872–77

Adams, Ann J. "The Birth of a Style: Henry Hobson Richardson and the Competition Drawings for Trinity Church, Boston." *The Art Bulletin* 62 (September 1980): 409–33.

Stebbins, Theodore, Jr. "Richardson and Trinity Church: The Evolution of a Building." *Journal of the Society of Architectural Historians* 27 (December 1968): 281–98.

7. BROOKLINE: 1874–82

Brown, Robert F. "The Aesthetic Transformation of an Industrial Community." *Winterthur Portfolio* 12 (1977): 35–64.

Elzner, A. O. "A Reminiscence of Richardson." *The Inland Architect and News Record* 20 (September 1892): 15.

Molloy, Mary Alice. "Richardson's Web: A Client's Assessment of the Architect's Home and Studio." *Journal of the Society of Architectural Historians* 54 (March 1995): 8–23.

Overmire, E. P. "A Draftsman's Recollection of Boston." *The Western Architect* 3 (February 1904): 18–20, etc.

8. EUROPE: 1882

O'Gorman, James F. "On Vacation with H. H. Richardson: Ten Letters from Europe, 1882." *Archives of American Art Journal* 19 (1979): 20–29.

9. STUDIO DAYS: 1880s

Bosworth, Welles. "I Knew H. H. Richardson." *Journal of the American Institute of Architects* 16 (September 1961): 115–27.

Janson, Richard H. "Mr. Billings' Richardson Library." *University of Vermont Alumni Magazine*, May 1963, 8–10.

10. LAST WORKS: 1882–86

Floyd, Margaret Henderson. "H. H. Richardson, Frederick Law Olmsted, and the House for Robert Treat Paine." *Winterthur Portfolio* 18 (Winter 1983): 227–48.

Friedlaender, Marc. "Henry Hobson Richardson, Henry Adams, and John Hay." *Journal of the Society of Architectural Historians* 29 (October 1970): 231–46.

O'Gorman, James F. "The Marshall Field Wholesale Store." *Journal of the Society of Architectural Historians* 37 (October 1978): 175–94.

————. "A Tragic Circle." *Nineteenth Century* 2 (Autumn 1976): 46–49.

Van Trump, James D. *Majesty of the Law*. Pittsburgh: Pittsburgh History & Landmarks Foundation, 1988.

ACKNOWLEDGMENTS

I WANT TO THANK THE FOLLOWING PEOPLE FOR CONTRIBUTIONS to my knowledge and understanding of H. H. Richardson and his work either through their writings or through their correspondence and conversation: Sarah Allaback, Paul Baker, Christopher Benfey, Geoffrey Blodgett, Robert F. Brown, Richard Chafee, Laura Cochrane, the late Anne Farnam, Margaret Henderson Floyd, the late J. D. Forbes, Elaine Harrington, Thomas C. Hubka, Robert M. Kline, Francis R. Kowsky, T. J. Jackson Lears, Michael J. Lewis, Katherine G. Myer, Paul Norton, Jeffrey K. Ochsner, Susan and Stephen Paine, William H. Pierson, Jr., the late Buford Pickens, Jack Quinan, Cervin Robinson, Richard A. Rothman, the late Ernest Scheyer, Guy Lacy Schless, M.D., Vincent Scully, George E. Thomas, Jennifer Thompson, Burke Wilkinson, the late James D. Van Trump, and Gary Van Zante.

A number of the architect's descendants have helped, including David Richardson, Heidi Richardson, Henry H. Richardson III, the late Joseph P. Richardson, Hugh Shepley, Roger D. Shepley, and a collateral descendant, the late F. Monroe Labouisse, Jr.

I am especially indebted to the generosity of the late Professor John Coolidge of Harvard University, who shared many of his basic findings and insights with me over the years.

My text profited greatly from the adroit editing of Constance Herndon. Cervin Robinson's photographs benefited from the kindness of Esther and Oliver Ames and Susan and Stephen Paine, the assistance of Elizabeth Felicella, and the hospitality of Helen Coolidge.